Check Your Relationships
Studies from Mark

by
Knofel Staton

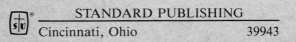
STANDARD PUBLISHING
Cincinnati, Ohio   39943

Unless otherwise noted, all Scripture quotations are from the *New American Standard Bible,* ©1960, 1962, 1963, 1971, 1972, 1973, 1975, 1977, and are used by permission.

"Turn Your Eyes Upon Jesus," By Helen H. Lemmel. Copyright 1922. Renewal 1950 by H. H. Lemmel. Assigned to Singspiration, Division of The Zondervan Corporation. All rights reserved. Used by permission (p. 12).

"Got Any Rivers," by Oscar Eliason. Copyright 1945. Renewal 1972 by Oscar Eliason. Assigned to Singspiration, Division of The Zondervan Corporation. All rights reserved. Used by permission (p. 69).

"Love Lifted Me," by Howard E. Smith. Copyright 1912. Renewal 1940 by Mrs. Howard E. Smith. Assigned to Singspiration, Division of The Zondervan Corporation. All rights reserved. Used by permission (p. 69).

Cover photos by Camerique

Sharing the thoughts of his own heart, the author may express views not entirely consistent with those of the publisher.

Library of Congress Cataloging in Publication data:
Staton, Knofel.
   Chech your relationships.

   1. Bible.   N.T.   Mark—Meditations.   2. Christian
life—Biblical teaching.   I. Title.
BS2585.4.S72   1987   226'306   86-23004
ISBN 0-87403-223-7

Dedication

This book is appreciatively dedicated to the trustees, administration, faculty, and staff of Pacific Christian College.

In Appreciation

This book would never have reached the publisher were it not for a typist. I am deeply indebted to Loretta Jane Skinner who typed the original manuscript and did not complain once when I would decide to rewrite some of it—after the typing was done.

Contents

CHAPTER 1

Turn Your Eyes Upon Jesus

Why Four Gospels?

I used to say, "When all the kids grow up, I am going to buy whatever cereal I want." But the longer I live, the longer the shelves filled with cereal get at the supermarket.

We live in a time of choices. Just buying a lawn mower these days can be complex. Will it be a non-powered push mower or a powered mower? If it is a powered mower, will it be a gasoline engine or an electric mower? If a gasoline engine, will it be self-propelled, one we push, or a riding mower? Will it have a grass catcher or not? Will it start by pulling a cord or pushing a button? Will the cutting height be adjustable or fixed? If adjustable, will the wheels be adjusted by having to take them off, or just by pushing levers? On and on the choices go—just in buying a lawn mower.

Aren't there days when you yearn for a more simple life with less choices to have to make? But life is made up of choices! And reading about the life of Jesus is no exception to that. When we decide to read about the life of Jesus, again we are faced with choices. Instead of just one writing, we have four—Matthew, Mark, Luke, and John. Why four? Wouldn't one do just as well?

Although there is but one Lord, there are many witnesses to that one Lord. No one person alone could capture all the gems of Jesus' life. John admitted, "Many other signs therefore Jesus also performed in the presence of the disciples, which are not written in this book" (John 20:30). John ended his writing by letting his readers know that no one by himself could completely capture Jesus, "And there are also many other things which Jesus did, which if they were written in detail, I suppose that even the world itself would not contain the books which were written" (John 21:25).

Having four Gospels instead of one serves us in many different ways. Here are at least three of those ways:

1. *Having four Gospels gives us something we can handle in our reading time.* Each Gospel gives us snapshots of Jesus written in brevity. That can encourage a person to pick up a Gospel and read it through. How many people would read the life of Jesus if it were written in such detail that it covered four or five thousand pages?

2. *Having four Gospels meets different needs of different people.* Each of the writers had a different audience in mind who had different needs. So the Holy Spirit inspired each of the different writers to meet those needs by sharing his witness about Jesus. Jesus is the Lord for all kinds of people with all kinds of needs. He did not restrict himself to just one category of needs. Jesus was indeed a man for all seasons.

Matthew wrote to a Jewish audience who was beginning to wonder whether or not Jesus was indeed the promised Messiah. No wonder Matthew took the genealogy of Jesus back to Abraham and no further. Matthew wanted the Jewish people who were questioning Jesus to know that He was of Abraham's seed. It was Matthew who connected more of the prophecies about the Messiah to Jesus than any other Gospel writer. Matthew, more than any of the other Gospel writers, showed that Jesus not only fulfilled Jewish prophecies about the Messiah, but also lived out an extension of Israel's mission.

Luke produced the longest writing, for the Gospel of Luke continues in Acts. As a matter of fact, that is really one writing that has been separated because of its length. Luke wrote to Theophilus, who was probably his friend and who probably had asked Luke a very significant question. Theophilus was a Gentile. Evidently, he was positive about the God the Christians were proclaiming, but Theophilus wanted to know who was correct—the Jewish people, who claimed that to be converted to God one had to become a Jew, or the Christians, who claimed that no people barriers, including race, stood in the way of a person's becoming a child of God.

Was the church in Theophilus' day performing or perverting the will of God by opening her doors to all kinds of people while the synagogues did not?

So Luke wrote in a way that shows that what the church was doing in his day in crossing all kinds of people barriers (the book of Acts) was a continuation of what Jesus himself began (the Gospel of Luke). Luke's Gospel shows that Jesus is the Savior for *all* kinds of people. Consequently, Luke took the human genealogy of Jesus all the way back to Adam, who was the father of all mankind.

Luke then showed more specifically than any other Gospel writer how Jesus crossed various types of people barriers. For instance, only Luke told us about the "good" samaritan, the rich man and Lazarus, Zachaeus, and the prodigal son. All of those people were considered untouchable. Luke showed that in Jesus, the untouchables are quite touchable, for Jesus is the Savior for all kinds of people.

John wrote his Gospel toward the end of the first century, when it was becoming extremely tough for Christians to hang in there because of severe persecutions. So John wrote several encouraging words to Christians in those days. He wrote the Book of Revelation to show that there is victory in Jesus regardless of the present circumstances. He wrote 1 John to outline for Christians what their relationship toward one another ought to be in the midst of trying times. And he wrote the Gospel of John to show Christians what kind of personal relationship with Jesus they could and should have.

It is very easy to turn our Christianity into a relationship with traditions, rituals, institutions, doctrines, and creeds. Evidently, some Christians were beginning to do that toward the end of the first century. So John wrote a Gospel that was really saying, "Turn your eyes upon Jesus. Remember that Christianity comes out of a personal relationship with the person Jesus, and it is supposed to grow into Christlikeness."

John centered his Gospel around the truth that Jesus is the vine and we are branches connected to that vine. The purpose of a branch is to carry inside of it all the characteristics that are inside the vine. Jesus says, "Abide in Me." To "abide in Me" is to abide in the *person* of Jesus, not just the *plan*. The Gospel of John makes it clear that in order to have and maintain that intimate personal relationship with Jesus, Christians have God's Holy Spirit (John 14—16).

To walk through the pages of the Gospel of John is to look into a mirror and see what the characteristics are that are inside the vine that God wants to flow through the branches—us Christians. So John not only reminds us about Jesus' characteristics, but also of the kind of people we can become in Jesus.

We will look at what Mark developed momentarily.

3. Having four Gospels gives us a check and balance system. If only one person wrote about the life of Jesus, we might ask many questions: Are his facts correct? Did he write from a personal bias? Is he writing about his feelings (what he wished had happened), or about facts (what really did happen)? Having several eyewitnesses to the same event helps to assure us of the reality of that event. Matthew, Mark, Luke, and John do not compete against each other; they complement each other.

Of course, there is a lot of overlap in what they have said (particularly Matthew, Mark, and Luke). That is not because they were copying from one another, however, but because they were writing about the same person—Jesus.

Each of them wrote while people who had heard, seen, and touched Jesus were still alive. Consequently, if they wrote error, the other witnesses around would have rejected their writing. They would have said such things as, "That's not true! I was there in person, and I know." But that did not happen. The early Christians circulated these writings all over the world, for they were accurate. They were life-changing. They were powerful— and they still are!

The differences in Matthew, Mark, Luke, and John are not contradictions, but rather augmentations of what others wrote for the purpose of stressing a different point. It is in those differences that various needs of people are met. We will look at some differences in Mark—that is, what Mark included in his Gospel that none of the other writers included—and see the significant impact of that on individual lives then and still today.

Why the Gospel of Mark?

Mark was writing as a pastor to some hurting people. While Matthew was writing first of all to a Jewish audience and Luke first of all to one person named Theophilus and John to a widespread general Christian audience, Mark was writing first of all to Christians in the city of Rome, most of whom were Gentiles. (The fact that Mark wrote to Christians in Rome is affirmed by early Christian writers commenting on Mark, such as Clement of Alexandria and Eusebius.) Because Mark wrote primarily to Gentile Christians, he did not include Jewish law and customs as much as the other Gospel writers. When he does mention Jewish customs, he explains it to his primarily non-Jewish audience. For instance, when he mentions the Pharisees' criticism of Jesus' disciples for eating their bread with impure hands, Mark explains that custom for his first readers, "For the Pharisees and all the Jews do not eat unless they carefully wash their hands, thus observing the traditions of the elders" (Mark 7:1-3).

But why is what Mark wrote to Gentile Christians in Rome in the 60s significant for us today? The answer is clear—most of us are Gentile Christians who are living in a Rome now or will be living in a Rome someday.

Our Rome could be within our immediate family. It could be at the place where we work. It could be in our neighborhood. In some senses, our Rome is the mass media of television, movies, and newspapers. In a real sense, the moment we walk out of a church building, we enter into a Rome.

To live in Rome as a Christian in the 60s meant to live in an environment of uncertainty, seen by the fact that sometimes Rome was tolerant to Christians and at other times severely intolerant. That caused the Christians to live in an atmosphere of insecurity and unpopularity. They were not insecure in Christ, but insecure in their culture. Their culture did not go along with the life-style, mind-set, and priorities of Christians. The atmosphere the Christians breathed was counter to the Christian's way of life.

Isn't that the kind of atmosphere we breathe today? Homosexuality, abortion, incest, cohabitation, nudity on the screen, and pornography are all increasing. And when Christians speak up against it, we are too often labeled as narrow-minded, not with it, unsophisticated, or barriers to progress. If we do not go along with the teachings of evolution, we are considered to be nonscientific.

The truth is that many Christians would like to take definite stands against issues in a community, but we do not. Why don't we? Why don't we speak out, sign petitions, have community meetings, write letters to the editors, or take some other action against abortion clinics, pornography, prostitution, and homosexuality? Is it because we just don't want the hassle that is going to come to us when we do that? Is it for self-protection? Is it because we know it would multiply our insecurity and unpopularity and we want to be more secure and popular in the culture in which we live?

Mark wrote to Christians in a very troubled time. And we are living in very troubled times. It is easy to take our eyes off Jesus and look more at the storms around us. There is a song that says,

Turn your eyes upon Jesus,
Look full in His wonderful face,
And the things of earth will grow strangely dim,
In the light of His glory and grace.

The "things of earth" do not refer just to material things that can detract us, but also the situations in this world that bring us trouble, pain, stress, and anxiety.

It is so easy when the storms are raging all around us and are aimed toward us to change the words of that song to read something like this:

Turn your eyes on the problems,
Look full in its terribleness,
And the face and the power and peace of Jesus will grow
    strangely dim,
In the darkness of all the doom and the gloom.

In the midst of the storm, it is easy to begin to wonder whether or not other Christians have faced what we are facing. It is even a temptation to wonder whether or not Jesus himself has ever experienced what we are experiencing. Mark's Gospel answers that need, too. Just what were Christians facing that motivated Mark to write to them this Gospel?

1. False charges of being anti-social: Because Christians would not participate in the Roman pagan feasts and other social affairs where idolatrous practices and immorality were common, Christians were charged with being haters of men and thus antisocial. It is indeed difficult to live in a community that looks upon you as a hater of other people in that community. There are some cults that appear to us to be that way. And we certainly do not want them in our communities. Many people in Rome looked upon Christians in that same light.

2. False charges of being immoral: Because both men and women met together in worship services in what many Romans considered to be closed and secretive, and because they would give each other holy kisses and seemed to be so committed to each other's needs during the week, many Romans charged that they were really meeting together for sexual orgies. It is uncomfortable to live in a community that has suspicions about your basic character and integrity.

3. False charges of terrorism: It was this charge that ignited a local persecution against Christians in Rome. In A.D. 64, a disastrous fire swept through the city and destroyed much of it. Only four wards out of fourteen were spared. The fire raged unchecked for more than a week and then broke out a second time after it had been brought under control.

The first rumors that were spread blamed Emperor Nero for purposely setting the fire. It was reported that his chamberlains were seen with fire torches and that gangs under his orders prevented anyone from fighting the fires. Opposition against Nero was hot. Nero tried to quiet the opposition by going all out in helping the homeless and injured. He levied a special tax for helping fire victims. He lowered the price of grain to provide food for the poor and ordered a massive urban renewal that cleared the slums, widened the streets, provided new parks, and insisted that all new construction be made out of fireproof materials such as brick and stone.

But none of this activity satisfied his opponents, so Nero turned the eyes of blame off him and onto someone else. Nero directly named Christians as the ones who set fire to the city of Rome.

Consequently, Christians were arrested and executed in horrendous ways. Many were crucified. Many were dipped in tar and attached to posts outlining sports arenas. Then, as people were watching the events, the Christians were lit to become the living floodlights to illuminate the arenas. Several times, Christians were the main attraction at the arena. They were dressed in animal skins, placed in the middle of the arena, and then animals that had been starved for the occasion were let loose to tear the Christians apart.

It was probably during this time that both Paul and Peter were executed in Rome. Mark had been traveling with Peter as his interpreter, so it was a tremendous personal loss when Peter was executed in Rome. But Mark's allegiance was not just to Peter, but to God and His people. So Mark wrote a pastoral Gospel giving encouragement in the midst of discouragement, giving hope to those who may have felt hopeless and some peace to the perplexed. Mark did that by writing about Jesus! And in that writing, Mark pointed out several different truths about Jesus that those people could hang onto. Remember, this would be the first writing about Jesus those Christians had ever received. When the remembrances of the persecutions pained them deeply, they could reread what Mark had written about Jesus.

Mark did not write a biography of Jesus. He did not discuss Jesus' parentage, birth, early environment, or many of the other details common to modern biographies. Instead, Mark began his Gospel with the words, "The beginning of the gospel of Jesus Christ, the Son of God." The word *gospel* means good news. So Mark began with a positive word—there is good news amid bad.

And where did that good news begin? It began in a wilderness experience. And that's precisely how the Christians in Rome viewed their environment—they were in the wilderness. But the wilderness can provide fantastic turnarounds that open the door to an everlasting future. No wonder Mark began his Gospel in a wilderness!

Do you ever feel as if you are in a wilderness—lonely, having little resources, uncomfortable, and somewhat confused? Then the Gospel of Mark is for you!

John the Baptist began preaching in the wilderness, and Jesus came to the wilderness *on purpose*. But out of that wilderness experience, Jesus opened himself up to the needs of others and entered ministry.

Mark immediately wrote about repentance for the forgiveness of sins and of people confessing their sins. Mark also made it a point to include, toward the end of his writing, Peter's explicit denial of Jesus (Mark 14:66-72).

Now how could those two truths minister to the Christians in Rome? Many Christians in Rome refused to admit they were Christians when that local persecution broke out. They did it for the purpose of saving their own necks. By the time Mark wrote, many of them were filled with guilt and wondered whether or not they could be forgiven of their denials. So Mark started his Gospel making it very clear that there is forgiveness of sins for repentance and confession. And he lifted up a hero to the Roman Christians, Peter, to let them know that even he had experienced the pain and guilt of refusing to acknowledge Jesus. He had done it for the same reason those Christians had—to save his own skin. Still, he had become a great leader in the church. He had found forgiveness in Jesus.

Do you ever fail to show your colors? Do you ever fail to stand up for something because you do not want to get knocked down? Do you ever cop out on Jesus in such a way that would

14

communicate that you are not a Christian? Is there life after denial? Is there acceptance for the backslider? Of course there is! The beginning and ending of Mark tell us so.

Do you ever feel as if a lot of people around you are against you because of your Christianity? They are "wild beasts" that would like to tear you apart. Christians in Rome faced literal wild beasts in the arena. But how about Jesus? When Mark recorded the temptations of Jesus in the wilderness (as we are tempted in our wildernesses), he recorded a fact that other Gospel writers did not report. Mark made it a point to show that Jesus "was with the wild beasts" (Mark 1:13). What a word of empathy to express to those Romans who had to face wild beasts. And when the wild beasts were not literal, they were symbolic, for many people acted like wild beasts. In fact, the term *beast* is one of the ways John symbolically described human opponents to Christianity in the book of Revelation. And Mark showed that Jesus continued to be in the presence of symbolic wild beasts during His life on earth.

Mark was saying to the Christians in Rome and to us today that they were facing nothing that Jesus himself had not faced, did not understand, and did not have compassion for.

None of the Christians in Rome had to face situations alone. Jesus was with them. While they may have felt helpless at times, in their midst was the Great Helper who had gone through similar situations. In fact, Jesus did not face the wild beasts in the wilderness alone. The angels were ministering to Him. I am convinced that God continues to send ministering angels to us in our moments, hours, months, and years of need.

Does this mean that we will totally escape physical danger in our Christian walk? Of course not! Jesus was eventually executed, but that was not the end of Him. He arose from the grave. His resurrection is the primary word of hope to persecuted Christians in Rome and to perplexed Christians today.

Mark wrote in a kind of style that not only encouraged his readers, but also motivated them not to sit around, worry, wring their hands, complain about the environment, and wait for better days. Mark was an *action* writer. Mark used the Greek word for "immediately" forty-two times—more times than in the rest of the entire New Testament. Every time you come across the word *immediately* or *straightway* or *forthwith,* then be reminded that Jesus is not just reactionary, but pro-actionary. He acts! He gets on with it! He does not allow the circumstances of His time to paralyze Him. He could easily have immobilized himself by negative thinking, such as, "I don't deserve all of this"; "I'm not going to expose myself to one other negative experience"; "God must be mad at me"; "I must have an inferiority complex to be getting all of this flack and misunderstanding"; "I must be unlikable for so many people to abandon me"; "I don't want to face another potential failure"; "I'm not going to act unless I'm assured of total success in the outcome"; "Silence is golden"; "Why rock the boat if I am in it?" He didn't do that!

By using the word *immediately* so often, Mark gave us the picture that Jesus was alive, active, and energized. He had purpose and intentionality—He was not going to allow anything to detour Him from a purpose that was far bigger than the circumstances surrounding Him. By this approach, Mark was reminding his audience to be active in doing the will of God despite opposition. When you get knocked down, get back up. If you are persecuted, don't act forsaken. If you are crushed, don't be perplexed. When you are literally dying for your Christianity, allow the life of Jesus to be demonstrated through your actions and reactions. Don't allow yourself to get paralyzed into inactivity. Have a bit more immediacy in your life on purpose for the Lord.

Mark also wrote a book that spotlights reactions. He picked up vividly the reactions of the audiences to Jesus. And those reactions were not all alike, and those reactions were not all desired by Jesus. Some people were amazed (Mark 1:27), critical (Mark 2:7), afraid (Mark 4:41), puzzled (Mark 6:14), astonished (Mark 7:37), and bitterly hostile (Mark 14:1). There are twenty-three different places where reactions are noted by Mark.

Whatever kind of reaction the citizens of Rome had toward Christians in their day, and whatever reactions the modern world has toward you as a Christian today, Jesus had the same reactions toward Him in His day. Christians can learn a lot as they read through Mark and notice how Jesus reacted to the reactions of others. Did He puff himself up when the reaction was good? Did He quit when the reaction was negative? He didn't even allow the reactions of others to interfere with His "immediacy" of action for doing God's will in the midst of His wilderness experience.

Who Was Mark?

Mark was the ideal person to write to these Roman Christians, many of whom had already denied Jesus and quit being

16

immediately active for Jesus. Mark himself had been a quitter. Mark had started out on the first missionary journey with Paul and Barnabas, but quit before the real work had begun (Acts 13:13; 15:38).

But Mark is a model that our Christian influence does not have to end because we have started and then backed away. Some Christians have been active in the church for a while and then dropped out. It is easy to think that there is no more room to start again. It is easy to be embarrassed by a new start after we have shown that we know how to fail. It is easy to remain a dropout. But we do not have to!

God is in the recycling business. Our Father specializes in forgetting the past and filling us with His presence for a new day today and a different future tomorrow. We must be willing to let go of those times when we disappoint ourselves, others, and God. The potential of a John Mark is in every quitter today! But that potential needs to be spotted and then tapped by someone else. In Mark's case, it was Barnabas. Barnabas saw potential in Mark, lit his fuse, and watched him launch.

Later Mark became a traveling companion with Peter and served Peter by being Peter's interpreter. He also teamed up again with Paul (Colossians 4:10; Philemon 24). When Paul was in prison and sensed that he was close to being executed, one of the people he affectionately longed to see was Mark (2 Timothy 4:11).

Mark had an interesting characteristic about him. That characteristic is seen by how he is described in Acts 13:5 and 2 Timothy 4:11. In Acts 13:5, he is called a "helper." That comes from an interesting Greek word, *huperetes,* which literally means an "under rower." The "under rower" kind of helper refers to the person who is willing to remain under the decks manning the oars while the captain of the ship gets the credit for its speed. The word came to refer to a person who was willing to help another person, willing to assist another person, willing to attend to the needs of another person. It describes a person who sees his relationship to others as that of service. He makes it a point to be knowledgeable concerning the needs and wishes of others and then deliberately seeks to meet those needs. No wonder Paul said that Mark was "useful to me for service." The word *useful* comes from the Greek word *euchrestos.* It is a relational term that describes a person who has adapted himself to the purpose of making someone else successful. He is the worker bee as opposed to the drone in the bee community. This word does not just describe a person who serves another, but also describes a person with good character who relates to others with kindness, gentleness, and friendliness. Such a person does not only get things done, but is also delightful to be with. Such a person is others-oriented, not self-centered. He gets his kicks out of seeing the benefits that others receive from his activity. He serves voluntarily because he cares about others. In fact, he loves others as he loves himself. He does to others what he would like others to do for himself. That was Mark, a useful under-rower helper.

Is it possible that one of the reasons we do not stick with a task is that we are too self-centered? Is it possible one reason we want to quit when the going gets tough is that we are too interested in the benefits we are not receiving? Is it possible that we cannot stand to be serving in the wilderness while others are enjoying the luxury of the castle? Is it possible that we do not want to be the worker bee, but the drone? Is it possible that we don't want to be the rower underneath the deck who is unnoticed and underpaid, but rather the captain on the ship who is having the banquets and getting the praises? Is it possible that we are more interested in being served than in serving?

Mark was a quitter, but Mark's commitment to serve others prevented him from remaining a quitter! And Mark was writing this Gospel as a service for others. He sensed the people around him in Rome were hurting, perplexed, anxious, wondering, and questioning. He did not cave in to some of the popular ways to relate to people in difficult situations. He never made any of the following statements, although we've all probably heard them said by someone sometime:

"You made your bed, now lie in it."

"You must have sin in your life, so God is punishing you."

"If your faith were big enough, you would not be having perplexities, anxieties, and questions."

"Cheer up, things could be worse."

"You've got problems—so what's new?"

"Just pray about it."

"It is what is meant to be."

"God loves those He punishes."

"Your sins are finding you out."

"I'm not reacting like this in the midst of difficult times; why should you?"

"Quit acting like a baby and grow up."

"Good riddance to those who have quit. That's God's pruning."

"The quitters have just shown their true colors."

Mark did not say any of that! He was too committed to serving other people, meeting their needs and healing their hurts. He sought to strengthen the weak, mend the broken, lift up the fallen, love the hated, associate with the lonely, forgive the sinner, energize the tired, comfort the troubled, clarify the confused, give peace to the anxious, identify with the downtrodden, and rescue the drowning.

How did Mark do it with his pastor's heart? He did it by turning the spotlight on Jesus. How did Jesus act and react? How did Jesus live in the midst of the wilderness facing the wild beasts of His day? Many of the issues we face today, Jesus faced then.

Indeed, turn your eyes upon Jesus—and the things of this world will grow strangely dim.

CHAPTER 2

Whom Are We Neglecting?
Mark 1:1-8

The prophets had been silent for 400 years, but expectancy was in the air.

A few people knew that the Messiah had been born. Zacharias and Elizabeth knew (Luke 1:43). Mary and Joseph knew (Matthew 1:18-23). The shepherds knew (Luke 2:8-20). Simeon knew (Luke 2:25-35). Jesus knew (Luke 2:49). But none of those tried to outrun God. Their patience and trust in God allowed Him to function within His own timetable.

There must have been many times when that was difficult to do. As they looked at the mess in the world, surely there were times when they wanted to say, "Now, God, now; what are You waiting for, God?"

Many times the Bible outlines the value of waiting. God called Abraham, but Abraham spent years waiting to fulfill his mission. God called Moses, but he spent years waiting in the wilderness. God called the nation of Israel, but they spent hundreds of years waiting. John the Baptist was born with a mission, but waited. Jesus was born as the Messiah, but waited.

People in North America do not like to wait. We get nervous waiting for someone to answer the phone. We do not like lines at the checkout counter. Some people hit their horn the second a red light turns green. Is it possible that one reason many congregations have difficulties is because people are not willing to wait for the Lord? If things don't hop quickly, we want new leaders. Whatever happened to the kind of waiting that stresses prayer and personal maturity toward Christlikeness?

Both John the Baptist and Jesus had been around for thirty years, but both knew the power of waiting. What was going on during those waiting years? As far as we know, neither traveled very much building a wide base of people support for the right time to come. John probably spent most of his life in the wilderness. As far as we know, Jesus never got out of the Nazareth-

Capernaum area except once to go to the Passover in Jerusalem. But both were developing character and intentionality. After Jesus' visit to Jerusalem, we read, "And Jesus kept increasing in wisdom and stature, and in favor with God and men" (Luke 2:52). Jesus matured intellectually (wisdom), physically (stature), spiritually (favor with God), and socially (favor with men).

I think it was during those growing-up years that Jesus committed himself to fulfilling the little things in life. He worked in the carpenter shop. He may have taken care of His mother, for Joseph may have died while Jesus was a youth. He observed women working with leaven, the significance of salt being put on good meat, the priority that many of the rich had, and God's care for the lilies in the valley. No wonder He spoke with illustrations that people understood. No wonder He was able to crawl inside their hearts.

Both John and Jesus entered ministry with maturity in them. Perhaps that ought to be in our criteria today. But Jesus and John also entered ministry as younger men than many of those who were listening to them. And yet, it is interesting that no one criticized either John or Jesus because they were younger than they. Are we sometimes guilty of closing our minds to the teachings of those who are younger than we?

John the Baptist had lived long enough to know what was going on in the relationships among the people of his day. He had enough experience to spot counterfeit sincerity when he saw it (Luke 3:7, 8). He knew about the greed of people (Luke 3:11). He knew about the business tactics of some who dealt with finances (Luke 3:12, 13). He knew about the ethics of soldiers (Luke 3:14). And he was able to beam his preaching and counsel to the specific relational problems of people. John did it with both clarity and courage.

Mark began his Gospel differently from any of the others. Mark began by picking up the ministry of John the Baptist as an adult. I wonder whether John the Baptist would have found a ministry in our churches today? Would we listen to him, or would he be one of those that we purposely overlook?

Nearly every community has that section or those sections of the town or city that the church does not want to penetrate. Usually it is the extreme sections of the area—the lower lower class of people, or the upper upper class of people. Both of those are easily neglected.

We know little about John, but when we see him as an adult, he is not one of those whom many churches would go out of the way to evangelize. He seems to have lived somewhat like a hermit out in the wilderness. And when he came to town, he looked and may have smelled somewhat like an animal. He wore primitive clothing and ate natural foods. Who would want to invite him to a fellowship dinner with his roasted grasshoppers? Let's be honest, folks, how many would have John sitting on the platform of the Sunday morning worship services unless they covered him up with a robe or put a more acceptable outfit on him?

I wonder how many people have had their potential squelched because we see people differently from the way God sees them? John probably would not be popular among us, yet Jesus said, "Truly, I say to you, among those born of women there has not arisen anyone greater than John the Baptist" (Matthew 11:11).

Notice how Mark described John's ministry (Mark 1:2, 3):

(1) "My messenger"—that is, a messenger direct from God.
(2) "Who will prepare Your way"—a ministry of preparation.
(3) "The voice of one crying in the wilderness"—a ministry of preaching.
(4) "Make ready the way of the Lord, make His paths straight"—a ministry of readiness.

In those days advance men went ahead of dignitaries who traveled. Because the roads were so rough and rocky, these advance men would fill in the holes, pick up the rocks, and also verbally announce, "The king is coming! The king is coming!" People in villages along the way got ready for the coming of the king. They spruced up their areas. They changed their clothes. They lined the roadway.

The roadway for Jesus is not sod, but souls. The roughness is not holes, but unholiness. The stones are not hard rocks, but hard hearts. To "make ready the way of the Lord" is to make hearts ready for the Lord to be able to live inside and then shine outside of those hearts.

But notice to whom John came with his message. He came to people that we today might also overlook. He came to the religious people. When we think that the world needs to become better, who do we begin to think ought to change? Is it the religious people, or only the unreligious? Is it possible that those inside the church need much changing? We must not neglect the

23

changes that God wants to see go on inside the religious people of our day as well as He did in those days.

John came to the religious people of his day because they were the ones who did not think they needed to make changes. They thought they were already right. The person who thinks he is always right is the most obstinate person around. That kind of person becomes more of a competitor against God than a companion with God. Unchanging people are more in the way than on the way. In fact, those religious people who were not willing to change eventually planned to kill Jesus. And today, religious people who are not willing to change often kill projects, programs, and plans that could advance the kingdom of God. Unchanging religious people today are too often tied to their past traditions, to their property, to their commitment of past saints who dedicated an organ, pews, or other pieces of property.

Whatever is in our hearts that prevents the entrance of Jesus needs to be changed. Some valleys need to be lifted (discouragement, feelings of worthlessness, neglect, rejection); some mountains need to be lowered (arrogance, feelings of self sufficiency); and some rough roads need to be smoothed (removing rocks of misunderstanding, bitterness, and grudges).

So a person we might neglect came to the people we might neglect with the message we so often neglect—"change."

Both the people of Judea and the people of Jerusalem were coming to John. That is an interesting mix. Jerusalem was the seat of narrow traditional orthodoxy within Judaism. But the Jews in the surrounding area of Judea were more liberal. There were many rifts between the Jews in Jerusalem and those Jews in the outlying areas. Those rifts centered around conservatism and liberalism. Now that does not mean conservatism and liberalism over essential doctrines, but rather over opinions, traditions, involvement in other races, and the like. The most conservative Jews stayed within the city and spoke only in the Hebrew tongue. Those outside the city, however, became somewhat more attuned to the culture in which they lived. Each would claim that the others needed to change, but not themselves.

Don't we do the same thing within the church today? Don't we often evaluate whether or not a person is conservative or liberal by how he stands in relationship to us, rather than how he stands in relationship to God? We don't cuss out brothers or sisters. We just call them liberal or conservative.

People on both sides came to John, and they came with sincerity. After the masks were down, they knew in their hearts that changes were necessary; so they were willing to respond positively to John's message of repentance.

John called the pious insiders to change and to go through baptism as an evidence of that change, "a baptism of repentance." The word *repentance* literally means a change of mind. But it does not refer just to the way we think, but also to the way we act. The belief change is translated into behavioral change.

Repentance is both a turning from and a turning toward. It is a turning from Satan and evil and a turning toward God and righteousness. It is a turn from immoral practices and a turning to moral practices.

True repentance will always change relationships—relationships with God, relationships with self, relationships with others, and relationships with the things of the world. In fact, baptism signals that kind of relational change, for baptism communicates a new relationship with God (adoption), a new relationship with the past (it is wiped out), a new relationship with the present (the indwelling Christ), a new relationship with the future (hope), a new relationship with the people of God (unity), a new relationship with Satan (disengagement), a new relationship with self (new creation), a new relationship with the world (we use it, instead of abuse it), and a new relationship with sin (the past sins have been forgiven and we are committing ourselves to a new life-style of righteousness).

But baptism in isolation does not do any of that. It is Christ who does that. Jesus is the central doctrine of the church. It is easy to be convicted and committed to certain doctrines, but not convicted and committed to the person and power and presence of Christ. For instance, some people can know everything about baptism, but little about Christ. That is a serious mistake. That does not mean that baptism is not important. But it does mean that baptism or any other doctrine must not have more priority in our Christian system than Jesus himself.

In fact, what really changes a man's total relationships is the indwelling of the Holy Spirit. So John moved quickly to declare that Jesus would baptize people with the Holy Spirit (Mark 1:8). To be baptized with the Holy Spirit is to receive the Holy Spirit. It is to allow our lives to be controlled by the Spirit instead of selfishness. The Holy Spirit unites us with God, empowers us and recreates us into God's image. The Holy Spirit is the presence of Jesus living inside Christians (1 Corinthians 3:16; 6:19).

The Holy Spirit is another person that we can neglect. It is one thing to talk about the Spirit, but another thing to walk in the Spirit. It is one thing to claim the Spirit, but another thing to be controlled by the Spirit.

We are commanded, "Do not get drunk with wine, for that is dissipation, but be filled with the Spirit" (Ephesians 5:18). What does this mean? To get drunk with wine means we are so filled with wine that we take on the characteristics that wine produces in us. And those characteristics are demonstrative! To be filled with the Holy Spirit means that we are so consumed by the Spirit that we take on the characteristics that the Spirit produces. And those, too, are outwardly demonstrative. What are some of those characteristics? They are love, joy, peace, patience, kindness, goodness, faithfulness, gentleness, and self-control (Galatians 5:22, 23). All of those affect relationships. The opposite of love is hatred, of joy is bitterness, of peace is animosity, of patience is impatience, of kindness is ugliness, of goodness is meanness, of faithfulness is untrustworthiness, of gentleness is roughness, and of self-control is hotheadedness.

Whether or not we are filled with the Spirit is always measured by our relationships and reactions. Most of the problems that we encounter in our churches, in our work situations, and in our family lives do not come from having inadequate knowledge, but from inadequate relational skills. Few divorces happen because a husband or wife did not know something correctly, but because they did not relate to one another properly. Few church fights, fusses, and splits come out of inadequate knowledge, but from inadequate relational skills. I have heard of very few splits that came out of doctrinal issues. Most of them come out of personality issues.

Isn't it time that we evaluate how we are treating others? Are we treating them with God's Spirit, or with our own?

Of course, we goof it many times. But do we recognize we goof it when we do? Yesterday, I really failed the mark. I had written a book and had turned it in to the publisher two months earlier. As far as I was concerned, I had done everything they had asked me to do. Then yesterday, I got a call from the publishing company. They wanted me to write three more chapters. This request came in the midst of a very busy time in my scheduling, and I blew my top! I gave the person who called me a real tongue-lashing. Now folks, that's the opposite of what it means to be filled with the Spirit. Later that day, I called back to apologize, but the damage had already been done. An old Jewish proverb says that a man's tongue is always long enough to cut his own throat. But I have discovered that we usually cut someone else's throat in the process. Isn't it easy to forget that all things work together for the good of those who love God? I am now thankful to God that I was asked to add three more chapters to the book. I believe the book was greatly improved by the message of those three additional chapters.

Is it any wonder that Mark identified the "beginning of the Gospel of Jesus Christ, the Son of God" (Mark 1:1) with the ministry of John the Baptist, who promised that Jesus would baptize us with the Holy Spirit? God's Spirit is the essence of the good news of Jesus Christ. Most of our problems vanish when we permit God's Spirit in us to take control of our relationships, actions, and reactions. That is good news! That changes emptiness into fullness, impotence into power, hatred into love, despair into hope, fruitlessness into fruitfulness, and Christlessness into Christlikeness.

It is time for every Christian in every church to commit himself/herself to being filled with God's Spirit and to allowing God's Spirit to come out of our lives in the way we relate to the people around us. To be committed to anything less is to be committed to something less than "the beginning of the Gospel of Jesus Christ, the Son of God."

Do you want to get a practical handle on what that means? Then read Ephesians 4—6, but pay particular attention to the practical relational skills mentioned there. Read those chapters again, list the various relational skills you spot, and then adhere to the command of God, "Do not quench the Spirit" (1 Thessalonians 5:19).

Anyone who is not committed to living out his life according to God's Spirit is not even yet at the beginning stages of Christianity.

Whom are we neglecting anyway?

CHAPTER 3

Can a Tornado Be Harnessed?
Mark 3:17

As we have already seen, each of the different Gospel writers had a different slant. That different slant came out of his concern for people. Each Gospel writer wrote with real people in mind. As he thought about his readers, he was sensitive to the different situations they were going through and the different needs they had. So the Gospel writers were open for the Holy Spirit to use them to purposely write in a way that would meet those various needs.

Every preacher and every Sunday-school teacher should do the same. No one should just repeat a lesson word for word because it worked once. Each preacher and teacher should bathe his/her preparation in prayers for the people of the church or the class. As the preacher or teacher thinks about people and prays for them, the Spirit of God will surely cause that person to be sensitive in applying the sermon or lesson to some needs that people are facing in days like these.

That's why every teacher who uses materials such as this book or curriculum material should add to the content an application slant that would link up with some of the needs of the moment. Is the church facing a period of high unemployment, high death rate, high number of terminal diseases, high influx of new Christians, or high mobility? Is the church going through a change of staff members, internal struggles, or relocation? Is it being discriminated against by prejudiced groups in the community, such as the zoning committee? Is it being misunderstood and slandered by the larger community? Just what does the Word of God have to say to our personal and community situations?

Our God is a personal God! He sent His Son in person to minister to real persons! The history of God's relationship with man from Genesis 1 to the end of the book of Revelation is a history of how God personally applies His truth, His grace, His judgments, and His principles to the personal situations of real

29

people. God specializes in real people. God specializes in scratching us where we itch. He is an expert in massaging us where we ache. After all, He is the Father who loves His children.

And so it is not surprising that His Spirit would inspire His Gospel writers to write in a way that relates directly to the needs of their first readers.

One of the ways to determine just how a Gospel writer such as Mark related the "good news" about Jesus to a particular audience going through specific situations is to see what he included in his writing that no other Gospel writer included. Most of what Matthew, Mark, and Luke wrote is identical in content, but it is in the differences that we see the distinctive marks of each one. It is in those differences that we see how each writer touched his audience in a bit of a different way from the other writers. And it is in that touch that we see the situation those people were going through.

Sometimes those differences are very small, such as including the words "wild beasts" when recording Jesus' temptation in the wilderness. But just adding those two words brings significant empathy and potential relief to the Christians in Rome, as we saw in the first chapter.

In this book, we want to take a look at some of the other things that only Mark recorded. These things will not be found in Matthew, Luke, or John. We will find that in each of these, Mark was keenly aware of what his readers in Rome were going through and that he had a pastor's heart to reach out and touch them in their situation. We will also see that these distinctive marks of Mark continue to touch people today with application for life.

Have you ever heard someone say, "He/she will never change"? It is easy to assume that a person's basic personality, the way he reacts to situations, and the way he expresses himself are locked in for life.

The Christians in Rome who were going through persecutions were probably reacting to those persecutions in many kinds of ways. Some, no doubt, were handling it much as Jesus did on the cross. They were not retaliating, they were not defending themselves, they were not projecting blame on others, they were not mad at God, and they were forgiving of their persecutors.

But others probably reacted in just the opposite manner. They copied Peter's action in the Garden of Gethsemane: they drew their swords ready to cut off the head of anyone who came near. If they didn't draw literal swords, they certainly drew the sword of their tongue and lashed out bitterly against their opposers. Some, no doubt, thought the way some people today think, "I will not get mad, but I will get even." Others took another approach, "I cannot get even, for I don't have the firepower for that, but I am not going to take this lying down. I am angry and will stay angry at those people who are treating us so unjustly."

Few people are proud of themselves when they react violently (whether with the tongue or with the fist) against others. Quite frankly, violent reaction toward those who are treating us unjustly is an embarrassment to Christianity. That kind of reaction does not follow the steps of Jesus. It does not follow apostolic teachings, for Peter wrote:

Beloved, do not be surprised at the fiery ordeal among you, which comes upon you for your testing, as though some strange thing were happening to you; but to the degree that you share the sufferings of Christ, keep on rejoicing; so that also at the revelation of His glory, you may rejoice with exultation. If you are reviled for the name of Christ, you are blessed, because the Spirit of glory and of God rests upon you. By no means let any of you suffer as a murderer, or thief, or evildoer, or a troublesome meddler; but if anyone suffers as a Christian, let him not feel ashamed, but in that name let him glorify God. For it is time for judgment to begin with the household of God; and if it begins with us first, what will be the outcome for those who do not obey the gospel of God? And if it is with difficulty that the righteous is saved, what will become of the godless man and the sinner? Therefore, let those also who suffer according to the will of God entrust their souls to a faithful Creator in doing what is right (1 Peter 4:12-19).

One of the three times that the word *Christian* is used in the New Testament is here. And it is used to describe the kind of person who reacts to unjust treatment in a way that does not bring shame to himself or shame to the church. In fact, it glorifies God because it reacts the way Jesus did.

But that is tough to do. It is not so hard to react with gentleness and Christlikeness when we are getting negative treatment and we deserve it. But when we do not deserve it—that is tough!

One of the problems in reacting violently when we receive less than we deserve is that such reaction can become a habit for us. Eventually, we will begin to react negatively to all kinds of situations in life—whether those situations are really affecting us in an undeserved way or not. It is easy to fly off the handle when we don't get our way in life.

Do you know some people who always seem to have to get their way in order to keep them calm? Can those people ever change? Can God ever use them in significantly positive ways in His church and in the community without bringing embarrassment to Christianity?

Some of the Christians in Rome were probably wondering the same thing, for many of them had probably lost their cool when the persecutions arose. Is there potential serviceability after temper tantrums? Is there potential positive witness that can be done after a whole city knows the quarreling have-it-my-own-way attitudes of some people known in the church? Should such people just leave the church? Is there hope for the hot tempered?

Mark sensed that some of his people were asking that question because they were sick and tired of some of their fellow members reacting that way. So Mark, inspired by the Holy Spirit for the occasion, recorded something no other Gospel writer recorded. As a matter of fact, we would not know this truth were it not included in the Gospel of Mark. What Mark recorded took only nine words in the Greek (up to twelve words in some English translations of it), but those few words speak volumes for multitudes of people throughout the rest of time.

Mark was recording the names of the twelve apostles whom Jesus chose. When Mark came to the names of two brothers, James and John, he added, "To them He gave the name Boanerges, which means, 'Sons of Thunder'" (Mark 3:17).

Just what does it mean to be nicknamed sons of thunder? It means these two brothers reacted like living tornadoes when things did not go their way. They formed a human thundercloud that whirled around and around and produced loud noise (thunder) and potentially damaging activity (lightning). These brothers lived out the *Burger King* philosophy—"Have it your way." And they believed they should have it their own way—and only their own way.

It would be interesting to know all the problems, stress, and frustrations Jesus had to face because of the actions and reactions of these two brothers on Jesus' staff. They reacted like living storms so often that Jesus himself nicknamed them the sons of thunder.

If Jesus gave you a nickname that would pinpoint your dominant characteristic as it is being expressed today, what nickname would He give to you?

On a couple of occasions, we can see at whom these thunderclouds aimed their lightning bolts. On one occasion, they were willing to burn up an entire village because people in that village would not provide hospitality for Jesus and His traveling team. This was a matter of expressed prejudice. Jesus and His team were Jews, and the village was a Samaritan village. There was a tense racial prejudice going on between Jews and Samaritans. James and John could not stand anyone having prejudice against them, so they asked whether or not they should burn up that whole village (Luke 9:51-56). That does not seem to be the best way to "win friends and influence people" for Christ.

But how do we react toward people prejudiced against us? Prejudice really refers to pre-judging. So it does not have to be restricted to a racial issue, but includes any situation in which someone has jumped to conclusions about us because they have pre-judged us without really knowing us.

How do you handle it when someone criticizes you? How do you handle it when somebody suggests that you are incompetent? How do you handle it if you are a woman and decisions have been made for you to have no responsibility in the church? How do you handle it if you are a divorcee and seem to be locked out of any meaningful ministry within Christianity? Neither leaders in the church or members in the church are immune from making unjust conclusions about people based upon pre-judging.

How do we handle other people in the church who react like two-year-olds with regular temper tantrums to get their ways? Do we ignore them? Do we stay away from them? Are we afraid of them? Do we cave in to their wishes and whims? Do we allow them to have their way? Do we manipulate relationships so that they will eventually leave the church and free us from all of that tension? Jesus did not allow James and John to have their way. He rebuked them for their reaction and reminded them that they did not know what kind of spirit they were really made of.

Another potential lightning bolt occurred when other people were not conforming to the way James and John thought things should be done. On this occasion, James and John saw someone casting out demons in the name of Jesus, but that person was not in the same crowd (congregation, denomination today) as the apostles were in. So it was John, with lightning bolt in hand, who said, "Teacher, we saw someone casting out demons in Your name, and we tried to hinder him because he was not following us" (Mark 9:38).

What is wrong with that kind of reaction? Isn't that the way we are supposed to be? Shouldn't we be competitive against other congregations and groups of people who do not do everything the way we do it or believe in every jot and tittle exactly the way we believe? Shouldn't we try to win the whole community to our church? Should we ever pray for another congregation to grow and have meaningful penetration and ministry in the community? Shouldn't we hold special classes to show how other "Christian" groups are wrong and why we should have nothing to do with them? Should we ever participate in any of their meetings or offerings for the community? Should we ever come together and have a joint sunrise service or a joint Thanksgiving service? Is it possible that we have narrowed the family of God down to our group only? Do we think that unity means conformity? If we do, then we can have unity with no one. I am certainly united with my twin sister, but we are not in total conformity. I am united with my wife, but we are not in total conformity.

To the degree that we are not interested in other people's succeeding for Jesus because they are not in our own group; to the degree that threatens us; to the degree that we have a competitive spirit, we are like sons of thunder.

Jesus' response to James and John must have been shocking for them to hear—and it's still shocking for us to hear, for most of us have a tough time believing it and certainly are reluctant to apply it. Jesus said to them, "Do not hinder him, for there is no one who shall perform a miracle in My name, and be able soon afterward to speak evil of Me. For he who is not against us is for us" (Mark 9:39, 40).

On the first occasion, James and John were really comfortable in destroying people physically. On the second occasion, they were interested in blocking others' progress, lest they should become more popular than James' and John's group.

On the third occasion, these sons of thunder simply wanted all others to be seen as a bit inferior to them. They asked Jesus to promise to do them a favor without telling Him what it was ahead of time: "Teacher, we want You to do for us whatever we ask of You" (Mark 10:35). Doesn't that sound like some of our kids in their growing-up days? Jesus certainly did not say, "Sure I'll do whatever you ask." But He did inquire, "What do you want Me to do for you?" (Mark 10:36). And their request was indeed like a growing cumulus cloud that wanted to take over the whole sky. They just asked that Jesus give them the two top slots in the kingdom. It would be Jesus, James, and John. That's not much, is it? They just wanted to be given a slice of the trinity.

Notice, they did not ask, (1) "What more can we do for You?" (2) "How can we ease Your work?" (3) "What more can we do for others in Your name?" (4) "In what areas of our lives have we not yet allowed You to be Lord?" (5) "How can we be better team members with the other ten?" None of that occurred to them. They wanted to bypass all purposes and get right to the privilege—"Make us great ones who will be recognized as such and who thus can demand honor and service from everyone else."

Doesn't that speak to us sometimes? Are we interested in status or service? Are we interested in doing the services on the platform that get the applause and attention, or the services behind the scenes such as preparing the Communion trays, or volunteering to clean out the restrooms in the church building? Do we get upset if we do not receive recognition from the pulpit, in the church paper, or in some other public way when we do something? Do we get upset if our name happened to be left out of the list of thank-yous? Are we willing to open our homes to traveling teams of singers, evangelists, or others? If we have leadership capacities in the church, do we have to be guaranteed a certain size crowd before we will speak or sing?

Surely these last two occasions related to some of the experiences of the Christians in Rome. Those Christians were meeting in various house churches, and we know by reading the book of Romans that they were having a tough time accepting one another, particularly over the racial issue. Paul wrote in Romans many times that there is no distinction between the Jews and the Greeks. He wrote that because those Christians in Rome had been making such a distinction. It is quite possible that they had been hindering the progress of other house churches by their reactions, by the things they said, by their neglect, and by their failure to support.

It is also quite possible that those Christians who did not cave in to the persecutions, but continued to stand up for Jesus even though they were pained significantly, began to feel that they were greater and should have higher status in the church at Rome than some of those who acted more cowardly. So James' and John's question about high status would certainly speak to them.

When Jesus answered James and John, He said something that only Mark recorded, "Whoever wishes to be first among you shall be slave of all" (Mark 10:44). When Mark recorded that Jesus said, "slave of *all*," he was speaking directly to some of the problems of those Roman Christians. They certainly were not interested in being slaves of *all*. They were not interested in serving those Romans who were against them. How about us? Do we go out of the way to serve someone who does not like us? Will we reach out in meaningful ministry to people who have hurt us? Do we know some people who are holding a grudge against us or against whom we are holding a grudge? Do we look for opportunities to be of service? And if we are of service, do they have to know we did it? We could know someone in need and move to meet that need without their ever knowing that we did it.

Some of the Roman Christians were also not really interested in serving their fellow Christians who were of a different race and saw things differently from the way they saw things. Again, that is clear as we read through the book of Romans. That's the reason Paul wrote to those same Christians that they should accept one another, but not for the purpose of passing judgment on opinions (Romans 14:1). He wrote to them that the strong ought to bear the weaknesses of the weak (Romans 15:1), that each one should seek to please his neighbor (Romans 15:2), and that their love should be without hypocrisy (Romans 12:9). Paul wrote that because he knew they were having difficult times with one another because of individual differences. So it is no surprise that the phrase *one another* appears in a letter to those Roman Christians more than in any other single letter in the New Testament. Paul wrote to those Romans these "one anothers:"

1. Be devoted to one another (Romans 12:10).
2. Give preference to one another in honor (Romans 12:10).
3. Be of the same mind toward one another (Romans 12:16).
4. Love one another (Romans 13:8).
5. Do not judge one another anymore (Romans 14:13).

6. Make for peace and building up of one another (Romans 14:19).
7. Accept one another (Romans 15:7).
8. Admonish one another (Romans 15:14).
9. Greet one another with a holy kiss (Romans 16:16).

Now ask yourself this question, "Are there people in my congregation for whom I will not actively engage myself in doing one of the items on this list?" If so, then you still have a bit of son of thunder in you.

The Christians in Rome must have had several sons of thunder among them. Some of the more coolheaded Christians were wondering what to do with those people. The sons of thunder among them probably had several different reactions. Some were filled with guilt and were uncomfortable with their situation. Some may have been questioning their own relationship to the Lord and wondering whether or not they were really Christians after all. Some probably believed that being a son of thunder was the correct way to show your colors and saw no need to change. Mark ministered to all of those when he recorded that Jesus nicknamed two of His apostles sons of thunder.

Did Jesus goof when He selected those two guys? Did He not know what they were like? Of course He did! When He chose one of the other apostles who asked Jesus, "How do you know me?" Jesus answered, "Before Philip called you, when you were under the fig tree, I saw you" (John 1:48). Jesus knew whom He was selecting. As a matter of fact, prior to naming them as apostles, He had spent much time with them. So why did Jesus include such rabble-rousers in His group?

Jesus saw potential in them and was willing to invest himself in tapping, equipping, and releasing that potential. And that investment paid off. The sons of thunder changed their spots. James, who was willing to fight back for just simply being rejected, was the first apostle to be killed, and he faced his death without a violent, retaliatory attitude. Instead of living his life by the spirit of the sword as he had been accustomed to doing, he began to live his life by the sword of the Spirit. John became known as the apostle of love instead of a son of thunder. He wrote more about love than any of the other apostles. It was John who recorded the words of Jesus, "A new commandment I give to you, that you love one another, even as I have loved you, that you also love one another. By this all men will know that you are My disciples, if you have love for one another" (John 13:34, 35). It was John who made it clear that bearing fruit for Jesus involves loving one another (John 15:1-17). It was John who recorded Jesus' saying, "If the world hates you, you know that it has hated Me before it hated you" (John 15:18). It was John who made it clear that one of the characteristics of being a Christian was love. That's a major thrust of his entire little letter of 1 John. It was John who said that if we claim to love God and hate (or neglect) our brother, we are a liar.

What a message for the Christians in Rome, who may not have been handling well their persecution. They simply did not have to continue their negative reactionary behavior.

But what will it take to change the sons of thunder in our churches today? It will take what it took in Jesus' day. There can be no fancy shortcuts. Barnabas spent time with Mark, and Jesus spent time with James and John. We must be willing to spend time with those whose conduct and reactions may be less than desirable. Jesus not only spent time with James and John, but also modeled what it meant not to be a son of thunder. We too must be living models whose examples make a difference with people in our presence. Jesus not only demonstrated a mature life-style, but also took a risk and gave James and John significant responsibilities while they were still sons of thunder. That may be the most uncomfortable risk for us to take. We like people to change entirely before we give them responsibilities, but Jesus knew that carrying out responsibilities could help a person become more Christlike. We also need to communicate with people in clear terms some of the characteristics in their lives that need to be changed, but we need to give them time to change and at the same time give them responsibilities that will cause them to know that they are indeed considered to be significant.

Jesus not only did the above, but also gave one-to-one instruction to James and John, as well as to the other apostles. We need to be willing to open up the Book and teach clearly the implications and applications of God's Word. We cannot just expect people to change from feeling only. The Word of God must be hidden more in our hearts and also transplanted more into the hearts of others.

Some historians tell us that John died at an old age—probably in his 90s. He became so feeble that he had to be carried to the church meetings. When he arrived, people would ask him, "John, do you have a word for us today?" John's reply toward the end of his life was always, "Little children, love one another." But people begin to tire of that repetition and asked him why he always gave the same message. John replied, "It is the Lord's command. And if this alone be done, it is enough."

What a change in character! What a change in perspective! What a change in practice! What a change in priorities! What a tornado harnessed!

The sons of thunder had indeed become sons of God. And so can we!

Just to record that James and John were called sons of thunder is a magnificent pastoral hope to every reader in Mark's day—and to every reader in our day.

CHAPTER 4

Are We Winning or Losing?
Mark 4:1-29

Is it really worth it? Is it worth it to get up early on Sunday morning and attend worship and Sunday School when many of our friends are sacking in—and that may be the only morning of the week we could? Is it really worth it to give a significant part of our income to the work of God through the local church in our communities? Is it really worth it to shovel snow out of the driveway and slip and slide to the church building for a special meeting?

Is the work of God on earth really making enough of a difference to warrant such an investment of time, energy, interest, and finances? Doesn't it seem as if the work of God is being overshadowed by all of the evil in the world? We are being told that the world is getting worse and worse and will eventually get so bad that the Lord will return just because the world is so rotten.

Is the kingdom of Satan outgrowing the kingdom of God? Just pick up any daily newspaper and browse through it, or listen to the evening news on television. Mass killings, serial killers, child molestation, the rapid spread of venereal disease, terrorism, warfares and fightings somewhere on the earth, and all kinds of violence abound.

When I was a boy growing up, life was surely different. We never locked our doors when we left the house. We certainly did not lock up tightly when we slept at night. We would not have thought about wasting electricity by keeping the lights on while we were away for a few hours in the evening—and certainly not have anything like a timer switch to turn lights on when we were away for a week or two.

Small children and women could walk the streets at night without any fear. The only thing I feared after dark was an imaginary boogie man, or possibly a ghost crouched behind a shrub ready to scare me.

Morality and immorality were certainly different in those days.

41

The closest I ever got to pornography was the ladies' section of the *Sears and Roebuck* catalog. About the only pills anyone took was aspirin, and people took that for everything. About the worst thing teenage troublemakers did was to turn over someone's outhouse at Halloween time. If someone was a real troublemaker—a social dropout kind of person—he waited until someone was in that outhouse before he turned it over. Sometimes teenage boys took a daredevil risk by buying a six-pack of beer and then driving way out into the country to experiment with being a big shot.

The sin centers in our town were the local pool halls. I was told as a boy never to go into the pool hall, and to my remembrance I never did. As I try to recall why the pool hall was such a sin den, I have a rather tough time putting answers together that are satisfying. There was no booze sold in the pool halls, for the whole county in which I grew up was dry. It was illegal for anyone to sell any liquor in the entire area. I suspect what made the pool hall such a notorious place was that the hall was filled with smoke and some vulgarity. However, vulgarity then was a different breed than vulgarity today. But to be any place where a lot of people were smoking and where talk was looser was considered to be too infamous for decent people.

Going to a movie was a different experience in those days, too. Everyone on the screen remained fully dressed. Any hint of sex was strictly that—a hint. Two people would kiss and then the screen blackened for a second, leaving everything to the viewer's imagination. I remember the day that I saw the movie, *Gone With The Wind*. And I remember hearing for the first time rank vulgarity in the theater, when Clark Gable uttered his now-famous line near the end of the film. Such language coming from the screen shocked the nation. I think many people returned to watch *Gone With The Wind* a second time just to verify for themselves that they really did hear such language coming out of the mouth of an actor.

But today, life has become so much more evil. At one time, advertising toilet tissue was banned on television. Now sanitary napkins bombard us nearly every hour in living color. Now even P.G. movies are shot full of vulgarity that does not even fit the plot. Sometimes I catch myself asking, "How in the world could any writer put that in? It just doesn't make sense, and it sounds so rotten." And the only answer that I have is that someone must put the whole movie manuscript on a wall and then stand back and throw darts at it. Wherever a dart hits, there goes vulgarity.

At one time, Christians became the main attraction as violence was done to them, and the pagans sat in the arena and got their entertainment by watching it. But now the situation is reversed. Now Christians sit in the arena of their living rooms, family rooms, and bedrooms and watch violence being done to others on television. And we watch it for our entertainment.

We used to listen to music on records that was delightfully wholesome. Frankly, some of it didn't make sense, like, "Mares eat oats and does eat oats and little lambs eat ivy. A kid will eat ivy too, wouldn't you?" But today, some of the words on records are absolutely, totally filthy. While some people claim that listening to that music does not hurt anyone, they are just kidding themselves. We would not think about walking in the alleys and digging garbage out of people's cans and stuffing our stomachs with it, but we voluntarily allow others to dump garbage into our minds and claim that there is no long-range damage from that.

As I am writing this chapter, the man police believe to be the so-called "night stalker" is in jail in the Los Angeles area. At night, he would break into peoples' homes and rape and kill women. His youngest victim was six years old, and his oldest was eighty-three. He had the entire Los Angeles area in fear at night. His favorite music album is *Highway to Hell*. (The album cover depicts a band member dressed as a devil.) His favorite song on that album is "Night Prowler." The song says in part, "Was that a noise out your window, or a shadow on your blind? And you lie there naked, like a body in a tomb, suspended animation as I slip into your room."

The officials have been told that the alleged night stalker listened to that song over and over again. He was obsessed by it. If the man they have accused really is the night stalker, then he eventually lived out the details of the garbage upon which his mind has been feeding.

Today, thousands of young people are missing from their homes across this country. It is quite clear that many of them have been kidnapped for the purpose of sexual molestation, and some will be exploited in X-rated movies. We now know that many of the scenes in such movies are not make-believe. What is being shown is the filming of live junk. We now know that many of those small children will never see home again. Many of them have been killed

43

following the filming. Others have been killed *during* the filming, for much of the violence and gruesome murder being done in X-rated movies is actual violence and murder being done in front of a camera. As I am writing this, officials are digging up the remains of victims who have died in such endeavors.

In the United States, nearly two million legal abortions are performed every year. As we continue that, we are more unkind than Hitler. During the holocaust, Hitler went after people who could run and hide. Remember the movie, *The Diary of Anne Frank?* The only "attic" for the protection of unborn children is the security of their mothers' wombs, but we have legally permitted intruders to come in to those security rooms and tear the unborn children apart. That is as cruel and as murderous as someone slipping into the bedroom of a baby and tearing that baby apart in the bassinet.

As we look at life around us, the question still haunts us, "Is Christianity losing ground or gaining? Does Christianity make a difference? Have we as Christians teamed up with the ineffective, impotent side?"

Those questions not only nag us today, but they surely tugged at the hearts of the Christians in Rome who were going through devastating times. Life seemed to be falling apart around them. It seemed to them that evil was triumphant. Surely they thought, "We have forsaken previous religions, changed priorities, walked away from immoral jobs, taken daring stands, been repudiated by our families, and sacrificed our possessions for the good of the church, but is any of that working? We wanted our Christian choices to make a difference, but is it really making a difference?"

Mark knew how some of these questions must have been gnawing on the people. So he picked up his pen and, with the inspiration of the Spirit, included something in his Gospel that none of the other writers included. He recorded this parable taught by Jesus:

The kingdom of God is like a man who casts seed upon the soil; and goes to bed at night and gets up by day, and the seed sprouts up and grows—how, he himself does not know. The soil produces crops by itself; first the blade, then the head, then the mature grain in the head. But when the crop permits, he immediately puts in the sickle, because the harvest has come (Mark 4:26-29).

Mark placed this parable after two others and before another. It is important to see how these four parables relate together.

The first parable tells about seed that did not produce a crop in two of the soils, but produced a bumper crop in one of the soils. What a realistic story! And its spiritual meaning is just as true as its physical. God's Word is not going to be productive in everyone who receives it. The Christians in Rome had seen that, and we see that today. However, when it does take, it grows into a bumper crop (Mark 4:1-20).

Some people want to keep their eyes on the negative side only— they like to talk about the failures of the Gospel. But the Lord wants us to keep our eyes on the positive. And keeping our eyes on the positive, we are to become spreaders of God's light. That's the gist of the second parable (Mark 4:21-25).

It is so easy to get discouraged in an environment that is filled with people who are not favorable toward Christianity. It is easy to quit after being rejected when going door to door calling. It would have been easy for the Christians in Rome to have gone totally underground to protect themselves. But there is "soil" prepared, and we Christians are to be planters of the gospel of Jesus.

What is the purpose of light or a shining lamp anyway? Its primary purpose is to cancel out darkness. Consequently, where should light be shining? There is no need for light unless there is the presence of darkness. So where the darkness is the blackest is where Christians need to shine openly and not retreat cowardly. We need to do that with both our content (what we say and teach) and with our character (how we live). We are told that we are to love what is good and hate what is evil (Romans 12:9). Standing for what is good in the community even if we have to do it alone is one way to let God's light shine. What do you ever walk out on? Ever walk out on a movie? Ever turn off the television because the values, scenes, and talk are rotten? Ever turn off the radio because the words to the songs are full of vulgarity and evil suggestions? Ever take a visible stand against pornography in your community? Ever speak out against racial discrimination? Ever attend a local school board meeting and speak against some literature or teaching that is present in the classroom? Ever attend the local school board meeting and take a stand for the permission of school facilities to be used by students to have Bible studies? Ever go to a city council meeting to take a stand for permitting the city to zone for some wholesome decision or take a stand against the zoning and permission of some unwholesome business?

Why do we so often fail to do any of that? Is it possible that we see the power, majority, concensus, and organization of those who take a different stand? Do we assume that we are so insignificant that our word or our life-style will not make a difference? Do we think the odds are stacked too high against us for Christianity to make any real difference? Then the next parable that Mark included has practical significance for us today (Mark 4:26-29).

Jesus taught in this parable that His kingdom would grow and *nothing* would stop it. So being involved in kingdom work and staying committed to kingdom priorities, principles, and practices is worth it. We may not understand exactly how His kingdom grows, but we do not have to know all of the inner details. The farmer certainly does not have all of the answers about how the seed that is planted sprouts up and grows (Mark 4:27). But growth in the right soil will happen (Mark 4:28). It is really the work of God. That's what Paul meant when he said, "I planted, Apollos watered, but God was causing the growth" (1 Corinthians 3:6).

Christians continue to invest in kingdom work despite what appears to be the growth of evil because they know that God is all powerful and that God causes work done for Him to spread, grow, multiply, and make a real difference in the world. Christians do it because they know that the one who is in them is greater than the one who is in the world.

There are several truths in this parable that every Christian needs to have rooted in his heart amidst the difficulties of his day. Here are some of those truths:

Kingdom Growth Is God's Business

Christians plant the seed just as the farmer plants and then waits for God to do His work. Regardless of the quality of the seed and regardless of the past success of other farmers, no farmer can have a crop without the provisions that God gives. A farmer did not even manufacture the seed that he planted. That seed came as a result of God's doing. A farmer never knows the potency of the seed he plants. That potency is God's plan inside the seed. The farmer cannot produce the climate necessary for a crop to grow to maturity. Only God can control that.

Growth Is Intentional

God expects His kingdom to grow. God purposes His kingdom to grow. The nature inside the kingdom is growth, as is the nature inside a seed. God does not expect His kingdom to grow accidently or surprisingly. Too many times, workers in the church do not really intend for any growth to take place. Too many churches are in a maintenance mode. No farm can stay in existence long if the farmer just keeps the machinery oiled, repaired, up-to-date, and in good working condition. No farmer is satisfied by simply saying, "We have a farm located in our community." No farmer worth his salt will refuse to be flexible or refuse to change because the newer methods are different from the way he farmed fifty years ago. Farmers have moved from the hand plow to the horse to the tractor. Some churches are so committed to doing things the way things worked many years ago that they are still in the hand plow stage. God intends for growth, and so should the church— leaders and followers alike.

Growth Occurs Amid Difficulties

Preparing the soil, planting, and watering take planning, time, and energy. As early as Genesis 3, God made it clear that we would eat bread "by the sweat of [our] face." Sometimes setbacks occur, such as hail storms, floods, or temporary drought, but difficulties do not mean that growth will be totally canceled.

Surely the people going through difficulties in Rome were wondering whether or not Christianity was destined to be destroyed instead of being allowed to grow. Some people reacted to difficulties by throwing up their hands and tossing in the towel. Others saw difficulties as challenges. Growth is enhanced when the challenges are faced squarely. Difficulties can cause us to do many things within the kingdom of God:

1. Spend more time in intentional prayer.
2. Recognize our interdependence upon one another.
3. Become more unselfish with resources.
4. Become more committed to priorities.
5. Set goals that are more specific.
6. Realize our dependency upon God.
7. Become less uptight with little things that at one time irritated us.
8. Major in majors and minor in minors instead of majoring in minors and minoring in majors.

Working through difficulties can better equip us for growth. No individual person grows without difficulties, and neither does a church. We began to eat by ourselves with difficulty. We began to take our first steps with difficulty. We began to run with difficulty. Few people first swam, canoed, rode bicycles, or played tennis with nothing but ease. Difficulties can expose us to the kind of exercise that can keep our spiritual hearts in good health. A life of total ease escalates the hardening of the arteries in the physical body, and also in the body of Christ.

When the first church faced difficulties after the day of Pentecost because many members did not have proper provisions, that difficulty solidified the benevolence of members toward one another (Acts 2:44, 45).

When difficulties arise, the best comes out in people and they rise to meet the need. Just watch what happens when a tragedy hits the church. People join together in a united positive effort. When the church in Jerusalem was persecuted and scattered, the people fanned out, evangelizing in a way that sparked tremendous growth (Acts 8).

Can't you see those early Christians leaving Jerusalem, their home? Can't you visualize them walking away from their houses and most of their possessions? Can't you see them walking outside the city as refugees with everything they owned on their back? It was not easy to leave their hometown and their houses. It was not easy to walk away from many of their relatives—mothers and fathers, sons and daughters who had not yet made a decision for Christ. They did not blame God. They did not question their decisions, but they did permit the difficulty to cause them to grow personally and cause the kingdom to grow universally.

Growth Is Continuous, yet Sometimes Unperceived

The growth of God's kingdom is like the growth of a seed. For a period of time, that growth is invisible. Then it breaks through the soil as an extremely small seedling, "First the blade, then the head, then the mature grain in the head." Few times can we actually watch the growth taking place. But we are able to discern the growth as we compare it over a period of time. That's the way people grow. We hardly notice our children growing on a day-to-day basis, but let someone who has been away for a long time see our children, and the first comment he makes is, "Oh, how they have grown!"

So it is with the kingdom of God. Sometimes we think that God's kingdom is not making much of an impact as we look at the mess the world is in. But don't compare what God is doing with His kingdom today with yesterday, but compare today with fifty years ago or a hundred years ago. God's kingdom is indeed growing. God's presence on earth is making a difference. Because of the compassion of God's people, we have homes for unwed mothers, Christian nursing homes, orphanages, hospitals, counselors, Christian schools and colleges, homes for the retarded, foster homes, prison ministries, campus ministries, new church work, new churches, hospital and military chaplains, more missionaries, relief in disasters, and the list of ministries and influences goes on and on. And they are making a difference. We are treating the mentally ill differently. We are treating people who are in prisons differently. We are treating the divorced differently. We are treating the alcoholics differently. Not only is our spreading of God's truth growing, but also our sharing of God's grace is growing.

If you get the idea that the kingdom is not growing, then just picture what the world would be like if the church had been absent for the past 2000 years. The kingdom is referred to as salt, light, and leaven. Growth is indeed inevitable and continuous, although sometimes unperceived.

Look at your own community and at people in the church. What would the community be like if no churches were present? What would families and individuals become were the church never available?

Of course we can see that evil has multiplied during the last fifty years, but also God's impact has multiplied. There are seventy-eight thousand more Christians in the world at the end of every day than there were the day before. Evangelism is becoming significant in many other countries, especially the third world countries. For instance, Korea is now a Christian nation, but that was not so fifty years ago. Many other whole nations are predominately Christian today that were predominantly pagan fifty years ago. The kingdom is growing.

Growth Requires Particular Methods

It is not enough to plant seed and then walk away from it. There are certain principles that a farmer follows in tending seed if the seed is going to grow. God expects us to follow His Biblical principles for the growth of the kingdom. As seed not only has to be planted, but also watered and cultivated, so it is with the kingdom.

The farmer who wonders why his seed under the ground is not doing as well as he thinks it should, who then digs it up to look at it, sees it has made some progress, and puts it back, will soon discover that the seed will die. We cannot be manhandling God's people, pulling them up by the roots with threatening comments, concepts, and conduct, then expect them to produce.

Plants need encouragement and so do people. We have even discovered that plants that are talked to or have soothing music played in their presence grow better. We cannot expect God's kingdom to grow inside of people or through people if we hold grudges against them, will not forgive them, will not communicate with them, and do not equip them for the responsibilities that we may be expecting from them.

Growth Requires Trust

While principles have to be exercised and hard work has to be done, growth of plants and growth for the kingdom never happen apart from trust. The farmer plants his seed and must trust. The farmer cultivates his crop and must trust. Too often people in the church spend too much time and energy not trusting one another.

I have discovered that people will do more to reach their potential if they think that we believe in them. What do people have to live up to if they think that we don't trust them?

One of the problems in church leadership today is that too many elders/deacons do not trust their preachers and too many preachers do not trust their elders/deacons. It is a shame when a preacher has to receive permission from several elders/deacons before he can make any decision on his own. If a church does not trust its preacher more than that, then it should get someone it can trust or change its level of trust in others. (At times, both may be needed.) No company can grow if its administrator has to call the board of directors together in order to make every daily decision, and no church can grow that way!

Jesus trusted His apostles. He trusted them enough to send them out on significant missions without His presence. He sent James and John with the other ten while James and John were still sons of thunder. But Jesus trusted them, and they lived up to that trust.

Of course, there will be times when we are disappointed in others. But that gives us a chance to help equip one another. It gives us a chance to manifest patience and grace with one another.

Growth Requires Patience

Anything that grows overnight will soon die. Parents must be patient as children grow. Farmers must be patient as their crop grows, and God's people must be patient as His kingdom grows.

We are living in the time of instant soup, instant tea, instant coffee, and instant cereal, but there is no such thing as instant growth of God's kingdom. With the Lord, a thousand years is as a day and a day is as a thousand years. God is not as hasty as we are. Just consider the thousands of years He prepared prior to the coming of the Messiah. We must learn to be patient—remaining under difficult situations without bailing out as we wait upon the Lord.

One of the most important teachings of God in the Bible is the teaching to wait. Moses waited in the wilderness forty years. Jesus waited thirty years from birth before entering into His ministry. Jesus commanded His apostles to wait in the city of Jerusalem after His ascension into Heaven. And they did not have the slightest idea how long they were going to have to wait, but wait they did.

Often, we are too hasty, irritable, demanding, fretful, and faultfinding because things may not be going as fast as we want. But let us be patient enough to live in God's eternity without demanding that the freeway pace and jet-plane speed determine whether or not His kingdom is growing.

Growth Means That Smallness Is Not God's Intention

That is seen particularly in the next parable about the mustard seed. It is time for us to quit glorifying smallness. God expects His church to grow and to grow large. Every individual congregation may not be large, but God's universal church is to become large.

Many congregations fail to grow because certain people in them want to keep possession of them. They want to stay in control, but if their churches grow, they will have to share control. Nowhere does the Bible say we are to be in control of His church. We are to be servers, not controllers. We are to look upon people for the purpose of taking care of their needs, not look over them for the purpose of supervising as superiors.

51

God wants His kingdom to become larger than any kingdom on planet earth (Mark 4:32). And He wants His kingdom to include all kinds of people in all kinds of situations. God's kingdom is big enough for the black and white, male and female, young and old, well and sick, rich and poor, Westerner and Easterner. His kingdom is big enough for various opinions of interpretation about Scripture. His kingdom is big enough to include all kinds of people who have been committed to all kinds of previous sins. His kingdom is big enough for the strong and weak, the stable and unstable, the balanced and retarded, the immature and the mature.

The church at Rome needed to hear that, for they were being persecuted. The persecuted could begin to think that pagans were not worthy of loving, serving, and evangelizing. The church where you are needs to hear that, too, for in every community, there are pockets of people that the church has intentionally turned its back on.

As a farmer grows his crop without discriminating who will eventually eat it, so the church must minister, live, and evangelize without discriminating who may eventually partake of the bread of life and eat of the Lord's Supper.

Growth Means We Should Never Be Discouraged by Small Beginnings

Most things that grow begin small in comparison to their potential. An oak tree begins as a small acorn. A person begins as a fertilized egg that cannot even be seen with the naked eye. The church that God commissioned to evangelize the entire world began with just a handful in Acts 1.

You may be in a small church today. Don't be discouraged by that smallness, but rather be encouraged by the fact that God's kingdom can grow and will grow if He has farmers who are not threatened by growth, who are not lazy in the face of growth, and who will put their hands to the plow and not turn back.

Rome seemed to be in a mess. Christians were persecuted, and discouragements must have been emerging. So it was common for some of the Christians to wonder whether or not God's kingdom was really growing. But those who doubted were looking only through a microscope and not a wide-angle lens. They were evaluating what they were going through at that particular time. If they could have had TV cameras to see what had happened with God's kingdom from the day of Pentecost, they would indeed have rejoiced with celebration of victory already in hand. For by the time Mark wrote, God's church had literally spread across the entire face of the planet and had included every category of person alive. God's kingdom was indeed turning the world right side up for a change.

Let us see the positive in the midst of the negative. Let us see the good in the midst of the evil. Turn your eyes upon the entire world. Compare it to what it was in the eighteenth, nineteenth, and early twentieth centuries. God's kingdom is indeed making a difference. The salt is salting. The light is dispelling darkness. The leaven is penetrating.

It is indeed worth it. But remember, the kingdom of God is not just out there. Jesus said, "The kingdom of God is within you." So let God's kingdom—God's rule—grow in your mind, in your heart, in your spirit, in yourself. Be open to growing.

That's the will of God. His kingdom can grow. His kingdom will grow. Indeed, His kingdom is growing.

CHAPTER 5

When the Pantry Is Empty
Mark 6:32-46

Difficult Days

As parents, you lie awake at night pretending to be asleep, but you aren't. And then you hear it. The front door opens and you sigh with relief, roll over, and can now go to sleep. Your teenager has come home and you know he/she is safe.

Then it happens. You hear some stumbling, and then a chair gets knocked over and you realize that your teenager has come home—drunk. You lie awake most of the night trying to put together in your mind what's gone wrong and how you can have a sensible discussion the next morning.

The next morning arrives and your other teenager, the one who stayed in all evening, greets you with a hug, a kiss, and a smile. She has been away visiting a friend for a couple of weeks and seems so glad to be home. While you two are having a bit of breakfast together, she then tells you why she has been away visiting her friend. She really left in order to have an abortion.

Your mind is reeling, fielding thoughts that come to you faster than you have ever realized they could, when your twenty-four-year-old son calls you on the phone. He calls you with some good news. It's about time you got some good news on this particular day. Your son lets you know that he has found the bride of his choice and is getting married. It is going to be a June wedding. That's a thrill for you, for you have been inwardly wishing that your son would find his dream and marry. Your son mentions he wants to bring his intended bride over to meet you later that afternoon. And you are dancing on a bit of cloud.

Later that afternoon, your son arrives with his intended bride and introduces you. The intended bride's name is Steve. And the wedding is going to be in San Francisco. You run to the den to see your mate, for you surely need to be held. As you walk in the den, you see an envelope on the desk with the words written on it, "I am leaving you. I am in love with someone else. Good-bye."

Life is falling apart. The storm has hit!

But that's not the end of life. There is still life to live, love to give, a God to serve, and people with needs.

It had been one of those super tough days for Jesus, the kind that makes you want to do nothing, think nothing, and go nowhere—unless it is just to get away from it all. Many of us know about days like that.

Jesus and His disciples had just received devastating, shocking, deeply grievous news. Jesus' special friend—that one who had asked nothing for himself, that one who drew crowds for Jesus, that one who had baptized Jesus—had just been executed.

But Jesus and His disciples did not throw in the towel. There is life to live, love to give, God to serve, and people with needs.

It was on that occasion that Jesus told His disciples to, "Come away by yourselves to a lonely place and rest a while." Mark added something to his report of that day that no other Gospel writer added, "For there were many people coming and going, and they did not even have time to eat" (Mark 6:31).

Isn't that the way it is with us many times? We get so pressed in with the needs around us that we can hardly take a relaxing moment. The Christians in Rome who had been going through devastating times surely knew about those pressure-cooker days when they may have gone far beyond the comfortable time for eating and resting.

Although it is difficult to get away, it is essential. And it is essential to do it at times where there is no telephone within miles. Those disciples did that kind of getaway, for they got into a boat and sailed "to a lonely place by themselves" (Mark 6:32). Only Mark mentions that they went to a lonely place by themselves. Mark knew his readers needed to hear that it is quite okay to do that. And today, we also need to hear that.

But while we are far away in those lonely times and lonely places, we should not build up a case to throw in the towel and withdraw from life.

As a matter of fact, before Jesus and the disciples got to that place, the crowds had gone ahead of them and were waiting for them. So what was intended to be a lonely place for them ended up being a hoard of people. The people were there with their needs, and they thronged Jesus and His disciples. They were not sensitive to the grief that was going on inside of those men. They just wanted their own needs met—right then.

Isn't that so common with us today? We may be hurting on the inside with many people around us—but no one seems to care about our needs for the moment. They are hurrying and scurrying and jockeying to have their own needs met.

Jesus could have got very upset by the lack of sensitivity on the part of the crowd, but He didn't. He felt compassion for them. And only Mark tells us how Jesus saw them. He did not see them as selfish people and scavengers just trying to get what they could for themselves in disregard of the grief and the need for some quiet time for Jesus and His disciples. No! Jesus saw them "like sheep without a shepherd" (Mark 6:34).

What a revelation for the leaders of the Christians in Rome to hear. For many of those leaders had gone through devastating times and needed some quiet time. But those Christian members who were being persecuted, chased down, and accused no doubt flocked to those leaders for help and teaching. It is so easy, as pressures pile up, to get irritable and just want to scream, "Leave me alone for a while!" Leaders need to hear Jesus say how they should look at others who come with their demands, who want attention, who want another's time, and who want to invade the privacy of others. See them like sheep without a shepherd, so that you can be to them a shepherd.

The function of a shepherd is linked up elsewhere in the Bible with the function of an overseer (Acts 20:28; 1 Peter 5:1-4). But many today misunderstand the New Testament's use of *overseer*. It does not refer to the supervising foreman who calls all the shots and who has to approve every movement. Instead, it refers to someone who looks *upon* others for the purpose of looking *after* them. It refers to those who care for the needs of others regardless of what those needs are. That's what a shepherd does with his flock. And that's what leaders are to do with God's church.

Those people who thronged to Jesus needed something for their hearts and, eventually, something for their stomachs. So Jesus taught them and then decided to feed them.

Using Little to Do Much

When He ordered His apostles to feed them with physical food, those men reacted much the way we probably would today. They looked at the number of the people to be fed—5000 men plus their wives and children (probably 15-20,000 people)—and must have shook their heads in dismay.

Philip must have had an accountant's mind, for he calculated the cost (John 6:7). While John says Philip came up with the cost factor, Mark says, "they" responded with the cost factor (Mark 6:37). I suspect that Philip was the first to figure it out and then quickly spread the news to the other apostles. Haven't you seen that happen in the church many times? A program, plan, or activity is suggested at a committee or board meeting. One person quickly gets out his calculator and figures the bottom line cost, and then just as quickly, he begins to tell all the other leaders how unaffordable the project is. In minutes, the event has been scrubbed.

Those disciples were convinced that the cost for bread only would have been two hundred denarii. That's a bundle! One denarius is equal to one day's wages. Just think about the average day's salary for the average member of your congregation; would you complain if the church decided to spend two hundred times that much money on one picnic?

Many people in the church today, including several leaders, seem to have graduated from the School of Philip. The first question they ask when any new idea comes up is, "How much will *that* cost?" And the question usually is not looking for a real answer. Regardless of the answer, the question is raised with the intent to scuttle the idea.

The cost factor, however, was not the only issue with the apostles. They knew that if they were to buy the bread for this crowd that they themselves would probably have to go to the nearest marketplace, purchase the food, transport it back, and then feed the crowd. In fact, the first part of their question was, "Shall we go," then the words were added, "and spend." Those leaders did not want to be inconvenienced with all of the extra work it would take to fulfill Jesus' request.

Doesn't that continue to stifle kingdom work today? Aren't inconvenience and cost the biggest issues considered? Just take a rather small item, and those two issues will come up. For many denominations, the suggestion to have the Lord's Supper every Sunday morning will be stifled because of inconvenience and cost. For those who have the Lord's Supper every Sunday morning, the very same issues are raised if it is suggested that the Lord's Supper be offered every Sunday night to everyone. That would be too much of an inconvenience for the people who prepare the Lord's Supper. And it will add to the church's cost. These are the first objections usually raised with little or no consideration to the fact that in the first century, there is no evidence that the Lord's Supper was ever offered just to those who were absent at the preceding meeting. That is not an act of unity, but of disunity. That's an act of embarrassment. We don't do the evening service like that for any other aspect of it. We don't suggest that the singing is only for those who were absent that morning, or the offering, or the sermon, or any other part.

Inconvenience and cost raise their ugly heads at most of the suggestions for ministering to people's needs.

This is the only miracle Jesus did that is recorded in all four Gospels. Surely God wants the integral truths of this miracle to come home to us. But do they?

The apostles had sized up the largeness of the crowds and the scarcity of the provisions and even suggested that a year's wage would not be sufficient, "for everyone to receive a little" (John 6:7).

Andrew came forward with five loaves and two fish. If a year's wages of food purchased would not be enough for everyone even to have a little bit, then what is the value of five loaves and two fish? Andrew probably didn't know, but at least Andrew was willing to offer to Jesus whatever he was able to gather, as insufficient as it seemed to be. We need more people who will graduate from the School of Andrew.

God needs more people who will offer to God what they have so He can use it the way He wills. Jesus is in the multiplying business. Instead of their not having enough for everyone to have a little, they had so much that everybody was stuffed.

Some women think ten extra people for dinner is really a chore (and it is). Think about a whole village of 15,000! If you dread the cleanup after a big meal, then you can surely feel something of the tension of the apostles when Jesus asked them to gather up the remains. Not only did they serve as waiters on that day, but also as bus boys who did the cleanup duties. If that kind of unassuming, unimpressive, low esteem functions were not too insignificant for apostles, then what is too insignificant for leaders in local congregations to do today? What should preachers, deacons, elders, and others refuse to do because it is too much below the dignity, education, and status of such leaders?

Only Mark records that Jesus had the crowd to recline in companies of hundreds and fifties. Perhaps Mark did that with the

Roman Christians in mind. Those Roman Christians had been meeting in house churches. Their companies were probably in fifties and hundreds, and they needed to be reminded that Jesus was quite aware of what was going on in gatherings of that size. And Jesus is able to meet the needs of people who have gathered together in small groups.

Notice some of the truths that come through this one miracle recorded in all four Gospels.

1. Jesus was willing to be inconvenienced by the needs of people at the very time that He really needed some quiet time.

2. When people came demanding more from Him, when He was already tired, when the day had already been long, and when He was grieving inside, He had compassion.

3. Jesus saw people with needs as sheep without a shepherd.

4. Jesus was willing to feed both souls and stomachs. We have no right to claim that only one of those functions should be the interest of the church.

5. Jesus thinks bigger than our excuses, and so should leaders today! Every time people come up with problems and excuses why those problems cannot be met, then leaders are to come up with creativity for answering those problems. God is creative, and we are made in His image! Mankind is fantastically creative. That is the reason there has been so much progress in the world in secular things.

6. God honors whatever amount we bring to Him. And He can multiply it! For instance, He might multiply it by touching the hearts of others to give when they see a desperately poor person in the church bring to the church a faith-promise commitment. The widow on Social Security who brings the amount of two or three months' checks for a special project might inspire a middle class or upper class person to give thousands or hundreds of thousands. God knows how to touch hearts by the motivation of others.

7. While five loaves and two fish seem like little, from the standpoint of that boy who brought them, it was much. It was all that boy had. God sizes up how much we have left over, not just how little we bring.

8. God does not see us as just a mass of people. He sees us as individual sheep with needs, and He relates to us best in smaller groups through Bible studies, fellowships, circles, discussion groups, and the like.

9. Jesus never pretended that the multiplication of the little was done only because of His ingenuity. It is easy to make people worship our administrative organizational skills when the unbelievable gets done. But Jesus looked up into Heaven and blessed the food and then divided it. He made it clear by that action that this was God's work through Jesus.

10. Somehow, leaders and members must quit using the classic excuses of inconvenience and cost. These two will always prevent God's work from progressing the way God wants it to.

11. No one in the church has a right to claim that any responsibilities are below his/her dignity. Those miracle-working inspired apostles did not delegate the nitty-gritty, tiring, humdrum arm- and legwork duties to people lesser than themselves. They did the waiting and the cleanup—and thus modeled something significant for us today.

Time to Pray

After this tremendously filled day, Jesus just had to get away. So He sent His disciples away in a boat and He went up into the mountain to pray. There are times when we must not allow anything to interfere with quiet time.

Notice that Jesus had a disciplined prayer life. He did not pray only when He *had* time for it. He *made* time for it. Jesus realized that if He did not make time for prayer that the following things would probably happen.

1. Emergencies would eat up that time. We can always find important things to do that cut into prayer time.

2. The demands of people would eat up that time. Jesus had to set times and places apart from the demands of people. And so will we if we take seriously the need to schedule prayer time.

3. Unfinished projects would eat up that time. Most of us have things on the front burner that need to be done.

Seldom will we find ourselves praying if we do not intentionally set time aside for that purpose—and then stick with that purpose. But we dare not fail to pray.

1. Praying regularly admits our dependency upon God.

2. Praying regularly permits us to be more honest with God by sharing with Him our innermost feelings.

3. Praying regularly feeds the inner self.

4. Praying regularly causes us to be sensitive to spotting God's answers to our prayers.

5. Praying regularly causes us to analyze our motives and goals in life.

6. Praying regularly causes us to be sensitive to the needs of others.

7. Praying regularly causes God to act. Many people feel that since God already knows our needs, we do not need to ask. But the Bible is clear that God responds to our prayers. In fact, God has even "changed His mind" about certain activities when people prayed (Exodus 32:9-14).

8. Praying regularly puts us into more of an awareness of the presence of God.

9. Praying regularly draws us closer to God's side. It empowers us for daily living.

Isn't it easy to set aside an hour for prayer and then think it has been totally fulfilled after about five minutes? And isn't it easy to run out of things to talk about with God? And isn't it easy for other thoughts to enter our minds concerning activities we just have to get done whenever we begin to pray? In order to help overcome some of these barriers, it is wise to order our prayer time wisely. Here are some possible approaches for ordering involved prayer life:

Approach #1

1. Thank God for everything that happened yesterday in order. Mention the items specifically and thank God specifically for those happenings.

2. Order the present day before the Lord with specifics. That is, go through every activity that you are anticipating for the day and bring that activity to the Lord in prayer, asking Him to be part of it, to fill it, to guide you in it, and to make that activity His activity.

3. Pray for your church in specifics. List leaders by name and pray for them by name. If you have a large church, then divide the leaders over seven days of the week.

4. Pray for specific ministries of your church by name. If your church is involved in several different kinds of ministries, then divide those ministries by seven days and spread the ministries out over the week.

5. Divide the world into different geographical blocks and then pray for the evangelism of one geographical block per day. Pray for the missionaries you know by name who are serving in those

blocks. You might divide the world roughly by continents, and pray for one continent per day per week: Asia, Africa, Europe, North America, Latin America, Australia, and other nations and islands of the Pacific. You could also divide the world into thirty major countries or regions and pray for a different country each day of the month.

6. Pray for the specific needs of people you know in an intercessory time with the Lord. Be specific. Don't just say, "God bless Mr. & Mrs. Smith." List specifically their needs and requests.

7. Then pray for your family members by name and about specific needs.

8. Finally, pray for yourself.

Approach #2

Spend an entire prayer time (forty-five minutes to an hour) doing just one main kind of communication. Here are some suggestions:

1. Thanksgiving. Begin from as far back as you can remember in your life and thank God for the specifics of your life up to the present.

2. Biblical remembrances and thanksgiving. Start with the beginning of the Bible and thank and praise God for the various activities He has done throughout the pages of the Bible.

3. Lifting up the greatness of God. Spend one whole prayer time just listing and discussing with God the various wonderful descriptions you can think of that captures something of God's greatness. Here are some ideas to prod your thinking: Rock, Fortress, Refuge, Eternal Bread, Living Water, Cornerstone, Friend, Father, Lover, Savior, Redeemer, Satisfier, Forgiver, Accepter, Adopter, Creator, Physician/Healer, Partner, Peacemaker, and Enlightener.

4. Spend a prayer time admitting to God various feelings, uncomfortableness, sins, ideas, and dreams that you have never actually spoken to Him about. Let Him in on your inner thoughts—on purpose.

5. Intercession—spend an entire prayer time praying for the needs of others without mentioning any of your needs once. You can pray for people, programs, organizations, churches, countries—anything but yourself.

6. Inviting Jesus in. All of our lives are filled with many rooms. It is important for us to invite Jesus into those rooms. For

instance, we all have a dream room, lust room, jealousy room, temper room, greed room, secret room, grudge-holding room, and more. Your inner self can be renewed by mentioning each of those rooms that you know you have, describing what is going on inside of those rooms, asking Jesus to come in and kick out the furniture that should not be there and putting new furniture in, making that room His living room.

7. Missionary prayer. Spend an entire prayer time praying for missionaries by name, country, and need.

8. Church ministry time. Spend an entire prayer time praying for specific ministries of your local church. Mention the ministries by name, the people involved, and the needs.

9. Evangelistic time. Spend an entire prayer time praying by name for individual people who you know are not Christians.

Jesus went up to the mountain to pray—and He invites us to join Him.

CHAPTER 6

When the Storms Come
Mark 6:47-51

The men were in the boat. That boat was being battered. The winds were contrary. They were a long way from shore, and they were doing something that Mark alone of the writers added—they were "straining at the oars" (Mark 6:48).

Doesn't that fit us? Our ship is getting battered with no letup in sight. Everything seems contrary to us, and we are a long way from harbor—from stability, from peace, from rest, from getting the answers, from getting it all put back together.

But there He was—walking on the water. What an unexpected time to see Jesus. And what an unexpected way! It was not on Sunday morning in church with the choir singing. It was in a mess of a fishing boat. The apostles were wet. Their hair was stringing down in their faces. Their eyes were stinging as the wind and the water kept forcing their way into them. Their muscles were aching as they were wrestling with the boat.

But that's where Jesus is! He is where the times are tough!

The ship was about to sink, but not Jesus. He is not going under. He walks through it. The storms come and go. But Jesus stays! Storms weaken, but Jesus walks!

Look at the disciples' reactions. They were out of their gourds. They were scared to death—not at the storm, but at Jesus, who was doing the impossible. And they did what we often do. They explained it away. In fact, they explained Him away, "It is a ghost!" they said.

They found human rationalization for permitting them to go on manning their ship without inviting Jesus in. But in the midst of their fancy explanations, their intellectual denials, and their egocentric independence, something happened. In a sense, they had been saying, "We can handle this alone. Letting God be a part of Sunday, yes! But seeing Him in the midst of struggling with life on Monday, no! It is a ghost! We don't need Him. Who needs Casper the ghost when the storms are raging?"

But in the midst of that came a calming voice. Through the splashing waves, through the roaring winds, through the crackling of the sails, through the stress sounds of the boards that hold the boat together, came that calming voice, "Take courage; it is I, do not be afraid."

Do you hear Jesus? He is saying, "I am in the storm with you. I know what you are feeling. When the waves hit you, they hit Me. When your face is stinging, so is Mine. But I am not sinking. I am bigger than the storm. I last longer than any boat—than your *family* boat, than your *career* boat, than your *health* boat, than your *financial* boat."

All of those can be threatened. All of those can get holes. All of those can go under, but not Jesus! Jesus was saying, "Believe in Me. Turn your eyes upon Me."

Then it happened. Only Matthew recorded what happened next.

> And Peter answered Him and said, "Lord, if it is You, command me to come to You on the water." And He said, "Come!" And Peter got out of the boat, and walked on the water and came toward Jesus. But seeing the wind, he became afraid, and beginning to sink, he cried out, saying, "Lord, save me!" And immediately Jesus stretched out His hand and took hold of him, and said to him, "O you of little faith, why did you doubt?" (Matthew 14:28-31).

When Peter said, "Lord, if it is You," he was not having doubts. The Greek reference to the way Peter said *"if"* was a statement of affirmation. He was really saying, "Lord, *because* it is You. . . ." We use that word *if* to refer to reality many times. For instance, we may say to someone who we know is going to the store, "If you are going to the store, bring back a tube of toothpaste." We are not doubting that's where the person is going, it is a way of stating reality. That's the Greek construction of the word *if* as Peter used it here.

So Peter was saying, "Because it is You, Lord, let me come to You." That's the heartbeat of all of us. None of us really wants to turn away from God when the going gets tough.

Peter, however, said, "Let me come to you—*on the water.*" Peter had guts! He did not say, "I cannot do that! I'll get in over my head. No one in my family has ever done anything like this before. The other leaders in the group will surely make fun of me."

Peter had a vision of a big God, and so he asked for something big. He did not say, "Jesus, if You will throw me a life jacket, I will swim over to You." He did not say, "Jesus, if you will create a row boat, I will row out to You." No! He asked to come on the water.

Then Peter did something beyond asking. It is easy for us to ask and then sit back and fold our hands. But Peter took a risk. He took a risk of faith. He got out of the boat. He got out of that boat of security. He got out of that boat of acceptability (after all, that's the acceptable way to stay on the water). He got out of that boat of traditions. He began to walk on the water. He was able to do that because he had a correct perception of reality. He perceived that God was big. That's optimism! That's realism! That's faith! That is real macho faith!

And then it happened. He began to see the storm. There is nothing wrong with seeing the storm. We are not blind. Of course, we see the storms that batter us. Not only do we see them, we feel them.

But Peter began to think that those storms were bigger than Jesus. Isn't that easy for us to do? We whittle God down when we talk up the storm. Sometimes, it is easy to think that in the boat without Jesus is safer than on the water with Jesus. No wonder Peter began to go under.

When will we learn that the storms are not in control? They will pass. All will pass. I have never known a thunderstorm to stay. I have never known a tornado to stay put. We must let the storms of life pass as we allow the storms in the atmosphere to pass, but we mustn't let Jesus pass by.

Peter began to sink. We know what that is like. Most of us have had those sinking, depressing times. Some may be sinking right now. But that is not a reason to throw in the towel. Many of us have had that towel in our hands with our arms uplifted to throw it in. But Peter kept his towel and his dependence.

When Peter was sinking, he didn't say, "I quit. There is no use. There is no way out. I've tried it and it didn't work." Nor did Peter go the other extreme that is so easy for us to do in the Western culture. That other extreme is to say something like this, "I'll get out of this all by myself. I'll swim for all I've got. I'm tough."

Peter didn't even pretend that everything was A-okay. He didn't play the big shot. He was honest and transparent. In a sense, he was saying, "Lord, I'm sinking and You're not. I'm scared and You're courageous. I'm lonely and You're love. I'm weak and You're strong. I'm little and You're big. I'm here and You are close by. Lord save me. I need help."

He went to the right source—the Lord. And he went with the right cry—help! He was willing to keep his hands uplifted in saying, "Grab me!"

Sometimes it is so difficult for us to admit that we need help. I suspect the next scene is a beautiful scene, although it is not recorded. How did Peter get back to that boat? I doubt that he walked on the water back to the boat. I suspect that Jesus picked him up and carried him back.

Isn't that a beautiful scene? The big brawny fisherman in the arms of Jesus on the water in the storm!

What was Peter's sinking problem? It was doubt. Jesus asked him, "Why did you doubt?" after he got on the water. God wants us to have faith in Him—even in the storms—even on the water, which is not created to hold us up.

Just what is faith? "Now faith is the assurance of things hoped for, the conviction of things not seen. . . . Without faith it is impossible to please [God]" (Hebrews 11:1-6). When God asks us to have faith, He does not ask us to push some special button that relates only to our religious side and our relationship with God. It is impossible for anyone to live five minutes without exercising faith. No one could take a drink of water without faith. He drinks in confidence of something he hopes for. How does he know there is not something in that water that would kill him? The only way he can know is to have that water analyzed. Then he has to trust the person who analyzed it. The only way he could do it otherwise is to analyze it himself. Then he has to trust the methods he was taught. Without faith, we would die of thirst. You cannot go to a restaurant and eat a meal without faith. How do you know the people preparing the food are not ticked off at the world and have decided to dump arsenic into the food? You cannot even get out of bed in the morning and put your feet on the floor, particularly if you sleep upstairs, without faith. How do you know someone hasn't decided to cut a hole in the floor so that as soon as you hit it you continue to go down?

Faith is a part of every activity we do. God wants us to give to

Him the kind of trust (yea, far more trust) that we give every other activity of life as we live through it moment by moment.

God wants us to trust Him even when the storms are knocking out our foundations and we feel like we are sinking; even when the storms are knocking out our walls and when we are vulnerable; even when the storms are knocking out our windows and we are getting hurt; even when the storms are knocking out our lights and we are in darkness. In the midst of all that, He says, "Trust Me. I am close by. It is I. Do not be afraid."

God does not promise that we will escape tough days. But He does promise that He is in the floating business, not in the sinking business. The water that may be threatening you is lapping around the ankles of Jesus like a puppy dog licking the heels of his master.

The song has said it well,

> Got any rivers you think are uncrossable?
> Got any mountains you can't tunnel through?
> God specializes in things *thought* impossible,
> He does the things others cannot do.

How did this day end? "And He got into the boat with them, and the wind stopped; and they were greatly astonished" (Mark 6:51).

Is Jesus in the boat with you? John tells us what is necessary for Him to get into the boat with us—"They were willing . . . to receive Him into the boat" (John 6:21).

Those disciples moved from their independence that explained Him away ("It is a ghost") to a dependence that invited Him in. And then, and only then, did they reach the harbor safely.

Is He in your sin boat? It is filled with holes and is sinking. Remember the song that we often sing, "I was sinking deep in sin far from the peaceful shore . . . sinking to rise no more. But . . . love lifted me"?

He can clean out your sin boat. But to do so requires that we confess our specific sins to Him and then be willing to turn from them.

Is He in your independence boat? Too many times, we just want to handle life by ourselves. It is tough to admit that we are too weak to get through the waters without calling in reinforcements. What is there in your life that you are handling all by yourself now? You need to give those over to the Lord and say, "Here, Lord, I've been manning this boat by myself too long. I want You to take over the controls." Sometimes our independence boat is really our control boat. We want to be in control of people, ministries, and activities around us.

Is He in your security boat? Peter was willing to sink for God. One of the problems that faces Christianity today is that we have too few people that want to get out of our security boats. We want everything worked out to our satisfaction and guaranteed before we make decisions. We want to take few risks. We can't think about the possibility of sinking. We don't like failures. There are several risks that you may be needing to take soon:

1. The risk of forgiving. Some of you may be holding grudges against those who have hurt you on purpose. It may be a risk to get out of your boat and go to that person with a heart filled with forgiveness and let the person know, "I forgive you and will never bring this up to you again."

2. The financial risk. Some have never made financial commitments to God's work beyond the "comfortable level." Most of us, at times, have bought cars that stretched the budget beyond the comfortable level. We have committed ourselves to making house payments beyond the comfortable level. We have taken vacations that stretched the money beyond the comfortable level. But when it comes to supporting God's work, we want to stay in our boat of security. Can you imagine the kind of progress God's work could make if His people were as willing to borrow money from the bank to get a significant project off the ground as we are willing to borrow for potential junk—like an automobile?

3. A ministry or service risk. Some people need to get out of their boat of security and risk reaching out in service to other people. That might involve something as traditional as teaching a Sunday-school class or as untraditional as working in an inner-city ministry. Some people need to consider using their expertise on a foreign mission field.

Jesus promised that if we are busy fulfilling the Great Commission, He would be with us forever. Isn't that enough to begin to take some risks?

Peter was willing to sink for Jesus. When we are willing even to sink for Jesus, then we will discover that we are walking *toward* Him. As we walk toward Him, we will soon discover that we are walking *with* Him. We will then discover that we are walking *for*

Him. And then we will discover that when the storms come, He will carry us. That does not mean that we will not have tough times. Storms are not comfortable to live through. But that does mean we are promised that He will be with us in the midst of those storms. Some people want the rainbow, but not the rain. Some people would like to experience the parting of the Red Sea, but do not want Pharoah ever to chase them. Some people want God to provide them the manna from Heaven, but they never want to spend time in the wilderness. Some people would like the experience of some special revelation from God as Paul had, but they never want to be stoned or put in prison. To put it in modern terminology—some people want to make touchdowns, but never be tackled.

Is He in your burden boat? Some are so burdened down that the boat is sinking, not because there are storms blowing outside, but because there is too much cargo inside.

Some need to let much of the cargo of their past be dumped overboard with the assurance that He who is able to walk on the water will be with us as we go through those waters. God said,

When you pass through the waters, I will be with you;
and through the rivers, they will not overflow you.
When you walk through the fire, you will not be scorched,
Nor will the flame burn you.

Since you are precious in My sight,
Since you are honored and I love you. . . .

Do not call to mind the former things,
Or ponder things of the past.
Behold, I will do something new,
Now it will spring forth. . . .

I, even I, am the one who wipes out your transgressions for
My own sake;
And I will not remember your sins.

(Isaiah 43:2, 4, 18, 19, 25)

Remember, when the storms come, the one who walks on water is close by. He is not sinking. He has never sunk, and He never will.

CHAPTER 7

What Is Our Priority?
Mark 7:1—8:21

Many years ago, a state legislator spoke at the morning worship service in my hometown. In his message, he raised an interesting question. He suggested that if someone broke out one of the windows in the church building on Monday, church leaders and/or church members would do whatever was necessary to insure that it was fixed by the following weekend. But then he raised the question, "If a boy's life is broken on Monday—if he is put into jail on Monday—will the church leaders and/or members do anything to help insure that the boy's life is put back together again before the weekend—or ever?

That question was asked over twenty-five years ago, and has nagged me ever since.

I am aware of how fast we move if a window gets broken out. I am not convinced that we are motivated to move at all if a boy gets broken—particularly if he is the wrong kind of boy—particularly if he is not already related to the congregation somehow—particularly if he is the kind of boy that no one else cares much about.

The Christians in Rome were going through devastating times when Mark wrote. It is so easy when times get tough for us personally to turn our priorities inward. It is so easy to protect self. And sometimes, in the midst of difficulties, it is tough to be sensitive to what is going on in the lives of other people and to make other people our priority.

In Mark 8:22-26, Mark records a miracle Jesus did that no other Gospel writer recorded. It is a surprising miracle. It doesn't take long to record. But the message in the miracle has a powerful truth that the church today still has a tough time seeing and applying.

In order to get the impact of the miracle, we need to see the steps that Mark laid down in order to get us to the landing of that miracle. Unless we walk on those steps, we will miss the landing.

And Mark wanted us to stand on that landing as a solid place from which our relationships with others are launched. So in this chapter, we are going to look at those steps in order.

Consider People More Important Than Traditions (Mark 7:1-23)

The Pharisees put Jesus on the hot spot, because Jesus did not keep all the ritualistic traditions that the Pharisees considered to be so important in order to be pure in the sight of God. Jesus and His disciples had been touching people who belonged to that wrong and dirty race. That itself broke the Pharisees' purified traditions. But that liberalism became even more serious as they dared to eat their meals without washing off all that filth.

The Pharisees were the religious Doberman Pincher guard dogs of the system. They watched every aspect to make sure that things went according to propriety. And "according to propriety" meant according to tradition—the way they had always done it. The scribes were the expert Scripture quoters of that time. They could pull out chapter and verse for proving that only their way was the correct way.

So they teamed up against Jesus. They were willing to argue even against God in flesh. If they were willing to charge Jesus with impropriety because He didn't keep all the traditions, then we should not be surprised to find arguments and fusses going on within the church-body over nit-picky things. It was really a charge of near heresy when the Pharisees and scribes asked Jesus, "Why do Your disciples not walk according to the tradition of the elders, but eat their bread with impure hands?" (Mark 7:5).

The word *tradition* literally means something handed down. There is nothing wrong with traditions as such. We are all the result of and work with what others have handed down to us. But there is something terribly wrong when traditions control our worship, our flexibility or inflexibility, our acceptance or rejection of people, our ministries, our plans, our programs, our relationships, our grace, our attitudes, our priorities, our openness or closedness, and our growth or lack of growth. When traditions stand in the way of our being God's ambassadors to people in need, then those traditions have lost their usefulness.

Jesus responded to the criticism of the scribes and Pharisees with His own criticism. He made it clear to them that they had the right talk, but the wrong kind of heart, and their worship was empty (Mark 7:6, 7). Why was their worship empty? The purpose of worship is to praise God, and in praising Him to be better equipped by God to serve people.

Jesus made it clear that those religious leaders hindered the practice of the commandment of God for the protection of their traditions (Mark 7:9). What is the commandment of God, anyway? Elsewhere, Jesus said that all of the commandments of God are summed up or fulfilled by loving God and loving other people. And when traditions get in the way of that, they are simply *in the way.*

Jesus put people above traditions. He believed that God created people in His image, not traditions in His image. That does not mean that Jesus had no regard for traditions, but He believed that Godly traditions should serve people. He also believed that God's people should be servants and slaves of other people in the name of God and not be servants and slaves of traditions in the name of maintaining the past. He believed that God had compassion for people, not for traditions. He believed that God so loved the world that He gave His Son—not that God so loved traditions that He gave us by-laws. He believed that some traditions had become walls that kept people away from God. He believed that unless these traditions were checked, some people would worship traditions and serve them rather than God. He believed that some people actually loved their traditions more than they loved people around them. He believed that some people had kept, taught, valued, protected, and were interested in saving traditions more than doing any of that for people. He believed that some had been so hooked to their traditions for so long that they actually thought that those practices of men were equal to the commandments of God.

The Pharisees had grown to love lifeless traditions rather than lively people. How about us today? What traditions are we committed to keeping in our church? What upsets us if change occurs? Check what would happen to your blood pressure if any of the following were done in your church:

a. Moving the Lord's table from the front of the worship area to the back.
b. Changing the order of the worship service where the Lord's Supper is served.
c. People raising their hands as they sing or pray during worship.

d. Moving the starting time of the worship service ahead or behind one hour for the convenience of people.
e. Adding another worship service to accommodate the crowds.
f. Putting choruses and hymns on overhead screens instead of using hymn books or vice versa.
g. Having a band or partial band—with some brass and drums accompanying the singing in the worship services.
h. Lengthening the worship services another half hour.
i. Singing some of the contemporary choruses as well as some of the older hymns or vice versa.
j. Watching the preacher grow a beard or ride a motorcycle.
k. Listening to the preacher read from a different version of the Bible.
l. Seeing the preacher walking to the platform wearing a robe—or not wearing a robe (if that is the custom).
m. The Lord's Supper being served to everyone on Sunday evening instead of just to the ones who were absent that morning.

Is it possible that we could keep all of the above in the way that we wanted them to be and still to be a church not sensitive to the needs of individual people about us?

From Genesis on, God demonstrated His concern for people. Jesus came in flesh also to communicate God's love for people. The Pharisees missed that. Do we easily miss it?

Just find any Scripture that would prohibit altering anything in the above list. I am not talking about change just for the sake of change, but some of the above might minister to people's needs. We live in a very diverse culture. That is why different kinds of music minister to different kinds of people. So allowing a bit of variety in our music can open the invitational door for other kinds of people to be touched by the fellowship and preaching of God's church.

We might minister to some people in the urban areas by adding an earlier worship service, for instance. One response could be "We are not going to add any worship service just for the convenience of certain people." However, that remark fails to understand how our present late-morning hour began in the first place in this country. Having worship services at a late-morning hour was done for the convenience of people. That gave farmers time to do the chores and get the buggy ready while the wife got a lunch ready as they all went to the church building, and many times stayed all day. So what began as a convenience for people we often will not alter for the convenience of people. Failure to do so is to see traditions as more important than people.

While some people have as their priority keeping the external things intact, Jesus was concerned about what came out of the heart of people (Mark 7:18-23). What Jesus listed as coming from the heart relates to how people treat people.

Too many times, our traditions are wall builders that keep people out. I used to be a part of an environment within Christianity that looked at people very critically. Beards were out, mustaches were out, sideburns below the ears were out, hair that touched a man's collar was out, T-shirts without outer shirts were out, wearing jeans to any church function was out, wearing shower clogs in public was out, a person who had gone through a divorce was out, women's sundresses were out, a dress shorter than two inches below the knee was out, shorts were out, any music with a rock beat regardless of the words was out, playing pool was out, going to a movie was out, and on and on. Are we really lovers of people—different people, diverse people, delightful people, confused people, searching people, poor people, rich people, black people, yellow people, *any* people?

Jesus' response to the Pharisees and scribes made it clear that He refused to see people and relate to people according to the traditional way. He would not allow the glasses they wore to blur the vision He had of people. After all, His vision of people was God's vision. Isn't that vision good enough for us?

Include the Outsiders (Mark 7:24-30)

A Gentile Syrophoenician woman came to Jesus asking for help. She was an outsider whom the religious leaders of that day wanted to keep on the outside. They considered such a person to be subhuman. In fact, they called such people "dogs."

The words that the religious leaders used for dogs referred to the larger dogs that nobody wanted and no one would care for. They were the outside dogs that were kept there. Those kinds of dogs survived on whatever garbage they could find as they roamed here and there. No one claimed them, because no one wanted them around.

Jesus responded to that woman's request in an extraordinary

way for that day. He began His response by saying, "Let the children be satisfied first." The "children" referred to the Jewish people. The religious leaders of that day, however, would have said, "Let the children be satisfied *only.*" But Jesus said, *"first,"* not *only.*

I wonder which way the Christians in Rome had begun to think. Because of the racial problems that were going on in the church of Rome (as seen in the Book of Romans), some of them must have thought that God loved their race only. Other Christians in Rome may have begun to think that God loved only the Christians in Rome and not those non-Christians who were antagonistic against Christianity and persecuting individual Christians.

Do we sometimes begin to think that God loves *only* people in the church, cares *only* for people in the church and will provide *only* for people in the church?

Jesus said the word *first* because that was God's plan from Abraham on. God planned to minister to and evangelize the Jews first so that through the Jewish people all peoples would be evangelized and ministered to. And that is precisely what happened! Jesus was born from Jewish lineage. All the apostles were Jewish. But Jesus gave to that Jewish group the great commission to go to all the world—all ethnic groups. The church began on the day of Pentecost with Jewish members, but they were told that the promise was also for those who were "far off"—the Gentiles.

Jesus gave that woman fantastic hope and a sense of value. He did that by using a different word for dogs than the Jewish people used. When Mark quoted Him, he used the Greek word for dogs (verse 28) that was an affectionate, kind, loving, and inclusive word. It was the word for the little house pet that people wanted, provided for, cared about, and gave some priority to. It was the little house pet that people would allow to sit on their laps. The children of the household made sure that these lovely house dogs were cared for at mealtime. They would take some of their food, wrap it in napkins, and throw it on the floor so that the little house pets could feed on the same food that the humans were eating.

When Jesus said this to that woman, I suspect His tone of voice communicated openness, compassion, warmth, invitation, and acceptance. It is clear that this woman heard that, for she did not walk away in disgust, but replied in a positive affirmation that saw hope where the Jews had given her despair (Mark 7:28).

Who are the outsiders in our communities? Who are those kinds of people that have yet to feel a warm, open, accepting family? Why haven't they felt that yet? What is there that prevents them from sensing that from us?

Quite honestly, I have had a warmer welcome in some supermarkets, bowling alleys, skating rinks, and garages than I have had in some churches. A few months ago, I was in Minneapolis and walked into *Wendy's* to get a baked potato. The manager happened to be taking the orders on that day. As I pulled out my billfold to pay for the order, he said, "Well, hello, Mr. Staton. Do you still live on Oakdale Street in Corona, California?"

I was stunned. I had never been in that part of Minneapolis in my life. I had never been in that *Wendy's* before. To my knowledge, I had never seen that man before. So I responded, "How do you know me?"

He said, "Oh, I have written to you many times, and you have never answered yet."

I knew that was wrong, for I make it a point to answer all of my mail the day it comes, or the first day I am in the office after I return from a trip. Several minutes later, that manager was walking through the dining room area visiting customers. When he came to me, I asked him again, "How did you know me and know where I live?"

Then he let his secret out. When I opened the billfold to pay the bill, my driver's license was exposed and he made it a point to look at it quickly and catch my name and address. He did that on purpose, because he wanted me to feel welcomed in *Wendy's* in a personal kind of way.

What an impression he made on me! I couldn't help but wonder, "How many churches make people feel that welcomed and wanted?"

Some do! We had just become members of this particular church two weeks before it happened. At the prayer time in our Sunday-school class, a woman shared her prayer request. She said that her junior-high son had just been suspended from school because he was caught with marijuana. She did not know what to do. She requested our prayers. The interesting thing is that she was a visitor to that Sunday-school class. She had come looking for the help of God's people with a distressing and confusing problem.

I thought to myself, "Woman, you don't know what you are

doing. This is a Sunday-school class, and we Christians purposely hide those kinds of problems from one another. We don't want anyone to know. Surely, members of this class will get on the telephone and begin to talk about that woman who lives in the community and her problem." But was I ever surprised! People reached out to her. It was obvious by their initial response that they were sensitive and caring and intended to include her in their circle of fellowship and resources of help. One person went up to her immediately after class and said, "How old is your son?" When she replied, the man said, "I have a son that same age. Could my son and I call your son, take him out for pizza, become a friend to him?"

And that's precisely what happened. Because of that friendship, that boy's life got turned around, and that family became Christian.

While the Jews had been accustomed to looking at a Greek Syrophoenician woman in one way, Jesus refused to allow their traditional approach to be His. He saw her as a person whom God loved, not as a person whom God's people had learned to loathe.

Fellowship With the Physically Disgraced or Embarrassed (Mark 7:31-37)

Being deaf and dumb was looked upon as a disgracing situation. It was indeed an embarrassing situation for those who were deaf and dumb. They were neglected. They were ignored. They were bypassed. Not only were they outside sound and speech, but they were also outside the sensitivity and sweetness of others.

But again Jesus refused to see people the way others saw them. He reached out and cared for those, because they were as much persons as anyone else who could speak eloquently and hear a pin dropped to the floor.

Be Creative to Help People (Mark 8:1-10)

Jesus was on the other side of the Sea of Galilee in the area called Decapolis when a great multitude of 4000 men plus the women and children had gathered to be with Him. What is astounding is that the last time Jesus was in that area, they begged Him to get out of there. Jesus had healed a mad man with demons whom those people had kept out of sight and out of touch. Jesus cast the demons that had been in that man into a large herd of swine. When the people heard how He cared about one man more than a herd of animals, and particularly when those animals belonged to them, they wanted Jesus out of their area completely. So what happened between then and now that caused the multitudes to come out and want to spend time with Him? Jesus had told that healed madman, "Go home to your people and report to them what great things the Lord has done for you"; and that man did precisely that. And as he told what great things Jesus had done for him, everyone marveled (Mark 5:19, 20). So now the crowds came.

Just what "great things" had Jesus done for that man? Jesus not only had just cast the demons out of him, but also taught him that people were more important than possessions. Healing one person deserved more priority than keeping 2000 pigs.

But was that just an isolated incident in Jesus' life? Did Jesus consistently believe that people were more important than possessions? Or for the purpose of saving possessions, could He make a lot of excuses for not reaching out and helping people in need?

Now the multitudes who had heard that healed man tell about Jesus were in Jesus' presence themselves. And they were hungry. Now they would see if Jesus believed people were more than possessions.

Jesus did what was characteristic of Him. He was moved with compassion for the needs of the people. Jesus wanted to feed them, but the disciples began to make excuses. They thought there were too many people to help. It was the wrong place for providing that kind of help. They could also have added that it would cost too much money to feed that many people. As a matter of fact, that was one of the excuses used at another time when 5000 men had gathered. Those disciples saw problems instead of people. And when they saw problems, they saw inconveniences to themselves.

Isn't it easy for us to first of all think of all the reasons we cannot move to meet people's needs in the community in which we live. Is that one reason we do not grow? Can we grow in number without growing in ministry?

It is interesting that the multitudes were now coming to Jesus because the needs of one man had been met, and he had told them about the compassion of this Jesus.

The church will not grow today by just keeping the doors open, the services going, and the bills paid. The church must reach out to minister to the real needs of real people in the community in which that church exists. And people have all kinds of needs. When the word gets out that your church really cares about people, then the church will grow. How can we read Matthew, Mark, Luke, and John and so consistently miss that Jesus made meeting people's real needs a priority?

Is it possible that one reason we fail to meet the needs of people around us is that we do not have the compassion of Jesus? Is it that we are not sensitive? I believe God's people are basically very compassionate and sensitive and want to be used by God as vessels for caring for people the way Jesus would if He were here in person. And He is here in person—in your person and mine—for the church is the body of Christ, and our individual bodies house His Spirit. If we have the compassion and sensitivity, then why don't we meet growing needs more often as a church body?

Is it possible that some congregations could be freed up to meet more needs by consolidating with sister congregations? In some parts of the nation, church buildings were built every three or four miles from one another in the rural areas. Why? Because in those days three or four miles was a long way on muddy roads with horses and buggies. People would come together in those meeting places to hear the Word of God *and also* to spend the day with their neighbors, for this was the only time during the week that they had fellowship with others off the farm.

But today, things have changed. Our roads are much better, our horses are much faster, but we still have church buildings three and four miles apart. In many cases, each church building owns its own property, has a parsonage, has a full-time paid preacher, has a secretary, and perhaps other paid staff. Some of those congregations can do little more than keep the bills paid for their on-site program. Would it help unleash the ability of God's people to meet the needs of others in the area—in the city—in the county—if several of those congregations consolidated? Let's suppose five came together. Instead of having five full-time preachers and five full-time secretaries, we could have one full-time preacher and use the other four to specialize in leading specific ministries that touch specific needs of people in the area. For instance, one preacher could be the minister of families, another could be the minister of youth, and another could be the minister of the divorced and singles. Each could use his specific gifts in a more concentrated fashion.

Why would we refuse to do that as people of God when people

in other activities are doing it in our area? When I was a boy growing up, there were five neighborhood grocery stores within four blocks of our house. Today, because of better transportation and other reasons, none of those neighborhood grocery stores exists. And no one complains about having to go an extra distance to a supermarket. Is it possible we would refuse to consolidate our churches primarily because we want to protect our own turf? Is it possible we would refuse to do that because someone in our family helped to build that church building? Are we more concerned about that than about the availability and resources of God's people being used to meet growing needs of people and to grow in evangelism and foreign missions?

People can again have our priority—if we are creative. The first characteristic we see of God is that He is creative (Genesis 1:1). And mankind is made in the image of God. Man is indeed creative. Just look at the progress that has been made in various fields in the past twenty-five years. That could not happen if man were not innovative. We are innovative about nearly every other experience around us. Let us Christians be more creative in doing the work of God out of our love for mankind than the non-Christians are creative in doing their work out of love for money and profit.

Choose the Sensitive Over the Sensational in Ministry (Mark 8:11-13)

The Pharisees were looking for the sensational. They wanted to see the extraordinary and talk about the stupendous. When they thought about the ability of God, they thought primarily about the wonders, conquests, and miraculous happenings that could come through the power of God Almighty. So in the midst of what Jesus was doing with people, they demanded a sign of the sensational.

What blindness those Pharisees had! Of course, it is true that God Almighty can do and does do the wonders, miracles, and stupendous unbelievable events. But the day-to-day way God works in this world is not so much by the sensational events, but by His sensitive Spirit, who motivates His people to reach out and touch the needs of people. That's what Jesus had been doing again and again. But the Pharisees missed the sensitive because they wanted the sensational. They asked for a sign. And yet, that is what Jesus had been giving them every time He included a person they excluded or touched a person whom they would not.

83

No wonder Jesus sighed deeply in His spirit (Mark 8:12). Surely He was saying within himself, "When will you catch on? When will it dawn on you that I am the Messiah? I am God in flesh. God cares about people. God loves people. People are His priority. You want miracles to brag about, while God wants mankind to bless."

We can be quick to criticize those Pharisees, but what impresses us most—people who testify about the sensational events that have happened in their lives, or the day-to-day behind-the-scenes people who reach out and care for others with their compassion, with their provisions, and with their time—and do it with the love of God as followers of Jesus?

Spread the Love of Jesus, Not the Leaven of the Pharisees (Mark 8:14-21)

This section began and ended with the Pharisees' blindness to the hurting needs of people. For them, traditions, rituals, cultural propriety, and provisions were more important than people. And it is so easy to be caught up in that kind of thinking.

So Jesus immediately told His disciples to beware of that kind of influence that came from the Pharisees. He was saying to them, "Don't go that way with your principles, priorities, and practices."

It is interesting that Jesus connected the leaven of the Pharisees with the leaven of Herod. What did those two have in common? Both were interested in self more than others. Both were interested in prestige more than people. Both were interested in status more than service. Both were more interested in being seen with the right people doing the right things than letting go of some of that in order to really take care of people.

Matthew told about wise men who sought Jesus. But it is interesting that those wise men also ran from Herod. The wise men could have turned Jesus in by reporting back to Herod (Matthew 2). We Christians today can turn Jesus away by letting the leaven of Herold spread through us. The Herods want to be seen with the company of the influential. Jesus spent hours with the outcasts such as prostitutes and swindlers. The Herods want to save only themselves and people of the same class. Jesus saved others—and intentionally reached out to all categories of people. The Herods think first about public opinion. Jesus feared God, not the world. The Herods remain in control themselves. Jesus is not threatened to allow God to be in control. The Herods emphasize status. Jesus emphasized service. The Herods demand their own way even though it may cost someone's head (such as John the Baptist's). Jesus was willing to give himself up on the cross for the benefit of others. The Herods influence people by power plays. Jesus influences people by compassion and love. Do we seek to get our way by various pressures we apply to people—or do we cave in to the pressures they apply to us? How do we handle such pressures as the following?

    a. Peer pressure—the pressure from close associates.

    b. Traditional pressure—the pressure to do things in the traditional way simply because it is traditional.

    c. Financial pressure—the pressure to act a certain way so that someone will not withdraw funds from us.

    d. The punitive pressure—the pressure to go along with an inferior program because we have been threatened.

    e. The elite pressure—the pressure to do something because influential people suggested it.

Jesus said, "Beware of the leaven of the Pharisees, and the leaven of Herod." Are we following Jesus' command? Or are we being influenced by that leaven? Worse yet, are we spreading it?

Whether or not we are will be seen largely by how we see other people and how we treat them.

Whether or not we can see clearly or are blind depends upon our outlook toward people.

That's Jesus' point in the miracle that He does immediately—that surprising miracle.

But we would never be able to fully understand the significance of that miracle without walking on these six steps that Mark laid down for us prior to that miracle. Are you hitting those steps? Are those steps now your steps? To place our lives firmly on these steps is to walk with Jesus.

Now go back and read again what those six "steps" are all about: Be creative to help people. Choose the sensitive over the sensational in ministry. Consider people more important than traditions. Fellowship with the physically disgraced or embarrassed. Include the outsiders; don't ignore them. And spread the love of Jesus, not the leaven of the Pharisees.

Tough, isn't it?

CHAPTER 8

The Second Touch
Mark 8:22-26

In the last chapter, we walked down six steps that Mark laid down to help us approach the landing of this miracle. Without those steps, it would be easy to miss the significance of what Jesus was teaching in this miracle. So if you have not read the last chapter, you might want to do it before reading any further in this one. Only Mark recorded this miracle of Jesus. It did not take long for Mark to tell it, but it has taken over 2000 years for the church to live it. The people brought to Jesus a blind man. Blindness in Jesus' presence was not new. There are two ways of being blind. One way is to be blind physically so that outer vision is blurred or nonexistent. Another way is to be blind inwardly so that perceptions or understandings are blurred or nonexistent.

The physical blindness refers to outlook. The inner blindness refers to insight. The steps that Mark took to lead us to this miracle show that Jesus had been dealing with one kind of blindness from Mark 7:1 on. Even Jesus' disciples had a blurred insight, as seen by Jesus' question to them just prior to this miracle, "Do you not yet understand?" (Mark 8:21).

Physical blindness was considered a curse in the Eastern culture of that day. Many people thought that a person was blind because either he had sinned or his parents had sinned. The disciples themselves raised that question to Jesus about another blind man (John 9:2).

It is certainly not a curse to be born blind or to become blind after birth, for the person himself usually can do nothing to prevent that, and it is not a disgrace to be blind in insight if we have never been exposed to the light of the truth. But it is a terrible disgrace to continue to be inwardly blind and not see people the way God sees people after having the eyeglasses of Jesus Christ for years and years.

God expects us to allow Him to remove the cataracts that blur our vision of people. That is what the surprising miracle teaches.

Evidently the blind man's friends brought that blind man to Jesus and begged Jesus to touch him. By that request, they were asking Jesus to see that man differently from the way others were accustomed to seeing him. They were asking Jesus to cross the social barriers and bring to that blind man a sense of importance, self-esteem, and value.

No one in that day wanted to touch the blind people. Close friends and family would, but religious leaders would not. If that blind man had been born blind, he had not been accustomed to many human touches.

The more a person is separated from others, the more he needs to be touched by others.

We are rapidly moving out of the industrial era into the information era. As the information era continues to expand all around us, fewer and fewer people will be in the presence of other people during their weekdays. We will be relating more to machines than to people.

A few months ago, I had my first encounter with a talking *Coke* machine. I had been away from home on a week's trip when I came across this machine. I put money in the machine and was surprised to hear a pleasant woman's voice, "Thank you for using your friendly talking *Coke* machine." The voice went on to list the available selections. After I had chosen one, the voice said, "Thank you for selecting a *Diet Coke*. You will enjoy the taste. Your change is _____ . Come back and visit your friendly talking *Coke* machine again." Having been away from home for a while, I thought that perhaps I ought to get a lot of change and just keep pouring it into that machine and listening to that pleasant voice.

Sometime later, I was on another trip and stopped in a supermarket in Arizona to buy some fruit and other items. As my items were pulled across an electric eye, a pleasant voice said, "That's $.49. That's $1.10." As this continued, I looked carefully at the mouth of the lady at the checkout counter and could not tell that she was moving her lips at all. I thought, "What a fantastic ventriloquist. She should be in southern California marketing that skill. That's the finest display of ventriloquism without detection I have ever seen." Then it dawned upon me that the checkout lady was not saying a thing to me. In fact, she couldn't care less whether I was in front of her or not. The voice came out of the cash register, and when I gave my money, another voice came from the cash register and said, "Your change is $15.65. Thank you for shopping with us." One of these days I am convinced that a mechanical arm will pull the items across the electric eye and there may be no need for a checkout person at all. We are being told that we will soon be able to shop via computer. As a matter of fact, that is being done now in many places. We will be able to designate a store and an item, push a button on our home computer, and on a visual screen be able to scan the various choices of that item we want. For instance, if we want to buy a stereo, we will be able to see the various stereos that store has as well as stereos other stores in the area have. We can then select which one we want by pushing the appropriate buttons, and the store can transfer the amount of money electronically from our bank account to pay for it. The items will be delivered to our home. All of that without ever having to encounter one person. We are also being told that eventually, secretaries will be able to do most of their work without leaving home.

What is all of that going to do for the potential growth of the church? We are being told that the church can have its finest hour of growth in such an environment. Why is that so? Because people are going to spend more time in the evenings and on the weekends purposely linking up with people. Various kinds of clubs, fellowships, and associations will have their biggest growth. That is because people need people.

During the agricultural era, when our roads were muddy, one reason so many people went to church on Sunday and stayed all day through a picnic lunch and playing horseshoes or crocheting in the afternoon was to visit with people.

People had not been able to be with their neighbors and friends during the week. And so the meeting on Sunday was a time to touch base with one another.

When I was a boy growing up in southern Illinois, the biggest single day was Saturday. The town was absolutely full on Saturday. Men, women, boys, and girls came to town together to do the trading. Why did all the men flock to town on Saturday? It certainly was not because men were more interested in shopping in those days than most men are today. It was because people need people. The men came with their wives in order to be able to spend some time with some of the other men in the area.

The church in the future that touches people by its open friendliness, its meeting of needs, and its personable welcoming and involvement will grow. The church in the future that depends more upon programming and cold institutional forms will not minister well in the high-tech society.

The church must understand people, talk with people (not just at them), and relate to hearts as well as heads.

Jesus was like that. When they brought that blind man to Him, the first thing Jesus did was to take that man out of the village. Why did Jesus do that? Think for a moment what would happen if Jesus healed that man amid the crowds of an entire village. Crowds would immediately throng to him. He would have flashing in front of him hundreds of people rushing back and forth. He would see dazzling colors. Some people could handle that well, but Jesus evidently knew that such an environment would bring fear to that man. Jesus wanted to bless him, not bewilder him. Knowing the man's nature, Jesus did not want to add to his difficulties with this healing. Jesus entered into that man's mind, feeling, and heart and ministered to the needs beyond just his eyesight need. We need to be able to enter into the minds, hearts, feelings, hopes, and fears of our people and seek to minister to them where they are.

That's one reason Jesus did not use the same method every time He healed someone of a similar disease. Sometimes Jesus simply spoke a word. Sometimes He touched. Sometimes He allowed them to touch Him. Sometimes He spoke a word at long distance and didn't come to the person's presence. Jesus knew how to be flexible because of the diversity of the people who were hurting all around Him. He didn't have the mentality that because it worked this way once, that's the way He was always going to do it.

Jesus also did something else that seemed surprising to us. He spit on the man's eyes. But by doing that, Jesus used a method that would bring that man a sense of hope. The world in that day believed in the healing power of spittle. We do that today more than we may think. Just cut your finger or burn it and watch your immediate reaction. Usually, you will instantly put that finger into your mouth to sooth the pain. Jesus could have been complex by explaining all the intricacies of what was wrong with that man's eyes and then tell what needed to be done. He could have touched him and explained all that was going on inside the malfunctioning eye, but Jesus was simple. He did not speak nor act above that man's knowledge. He related to him as a fellow person who cared about him. No superiority complex or snow job coming from Jesus.

Then Jesus touched him. A touch from Jesus and that man still could not see clearly. That's surprising—a touch from Jesus, and he was still partially blind. Then Jesus asked the penetrating question, "Do you see anything?"

The man was still partially blind. He saw people like trees. He needed Jesus' second touch. Why? In order to see people as *persons*.

Jesus' question to that man is relevant for us who have physically good eyes—20/20 vision. What do you see as you look at people everyday?

Before Jesus came, the people of God had learned to see other people as things, like pawns, like property. Society was depersonalized. Alienation and meaninglessness characterized their lifestyle. There were many blinders that kept people from seeing people the way God wanted them to be seen. Here are some of them:

1. There was the *class* blinder. Those in the upper-upper class wore blinders that made them look upon the lower-lower class as people whom God did not love. As a matter of fact, the upper-upper said that the poor people were enemies against God, and that's the reason they were poor. The poor people wore their blinders, also. They considered the rich people as rip-off artists, and the only reason they were rich was because they were dishonest and disobedient to God. Neither claimed that God really loved the other.

2. There was the *nationality* blinder. Jews considered Gentiles as barbarians, animals, and subhumans. A good orthodox Jew would not even walk through Samaritan territory lest he become polluted by touching the same ground that the Samaritans walked upon. Gentiles did not know that God loved them, for they got their clue about how God saw them through God's religious people.

3. There was the *sex* blinder. Males did not look at females as fully human beings. This way of looking at people was popularized by the Greek philosopher, Aristotle. He wrote that a woman is to man what a slave is to a master. He also wrote that a woman is really an unfinished man, left standing on a lower step of the scale of development, and that the male is by nature superior and the female, inferior.

Aristotle wrote that silence is the woman's glory. He did not think any woman should speak and be heard. That kind of thinking began to spread across the entire world. Even Jewish males adopted a lot of that Greek philosophy. Jewish men prayed every day a thanksgiving prayer to God for not making them a Gentile, a slave, or a woman. Women had a hard time experiencing that God loved them and saw them as whole persons.

4. There was the *age* blinder. The Romans had a law that said if a new baby were born and the father walked in and then left without naming the newly born baby, the baby should be killed. Romans thought that children were a nuisance and created more inconveniences than they were worth. Aren't we saying a similar thing today in our wholesale abortion practices?

Even the disciples on one occasion wanted to keep the children away from the presence of Jesus. Children did not know that God could see them as He sees adults. They did not experience the love of God as adults did.

5. There was the *vocational* blinder. The religious leaders kept people of several different vocations out of the synagogue, such as shepherds, tax collectors, pig farmers, and others. People in those vocations felt unwanted. For the most part, they were right.

6. There was the *sin* blinder. If a person was immoral, he was ostracized by the religious leaders of his day.

7. There was the *health* blinder. If a person was sick, it was thought that he was sick because he had done something against God and God was getting back at him. If a person had a fever, they let the brain boil. To bring healing would be to interfere with the judgment of God. Aren't we doing a similar thing today? Don't we hear it said that if a person has a physical problem, then he needs to be delivered of some sin to get right with God?

None of the religious leaders of that day saw that those people presented opportunities for demonstrating the love of God. Instead they augmented the guilt of those people. And too many preachers today are doing the same thing.

Into this kind of polarized, segmented, and insensitive society, God came in the person of Jesus, shattering those interpersonal blinders that would prevent us from seeing correctly. Jesus taught us that God sees people as personal creatures of His. And then Jesus demonstrated in both word and deed the good news of what God is really like. God is love!

Jesus showed that God cared for the common man by calling the poor to be His personal disciples. He showed that God cared for the sick by healing them. He showed that God cared for the social riffraff by going home with them, eating with them, and being willing to be crucified between two of them. He showed that God cared for the hungry by feeding them. He showed that God cared for the religiously unclean by touching them. He showed that God cared for the sinners by forgiving them and giving them praise when they ministered to Him. He showed that God cared for women by talking with them in public, allowing many to travel with Him and His team, and by doing for women everything He did for men—He healed them, raised them from the dead, cast demons out of them, and praised them.

Jesus saw people as God sees them, and so He loved them and served them as God would.

It is true that Jesus was like God. But it is also true that God is like Jesus.

Jesus touches us today so that He may continue to bring the love of God to humanity through us—that through us, people can be seen and loved as people. Our world needs the audacious demonstration of Christians loving like that! But that demonstration is directly connected to how we see people.

That man whom Jesus touched did not see people clearly. He saw them like trees. To see people like trees is to treat them like trees. It is to see that they have life, but no feelings that need to be soothed. That's like a tree. I have never tried to soothe any feelings of trees. It is to see that people have life, but no souls to save. I have never spent any time preaching to a tree to get a tree to repent and give itself to the Lord. That may sound silly, but have you spent any time talking to someone about faith, repentance, and commitment to the Lord? If not, then you may be seeing them more like trees than people who have souls that need to be saved. To see people like trees is to see them with life, but without need of friends with whom to share. Are you open to taking the risk of sharing yourself as a friend with others, or is it more comfortable and secure to stay within your own sheltered existence and keep the newcomers at a distance?

Why could that man not see people correctly after Jesus' touch? We don't know; this is the only recorded miracle that did not provide instant full recovery. Maybe Jesus wanted to illustrate our own difficulty in seeing people correctly after we have been touched by Jesus. That man had a physical sight problem, but we often have a spiritual sight problem. We can't escape from our traditional and accepted ways of seeing people to see them as Jesus sees them.

Do we see people according to the customary, expected, and acceptable ways and then treat them in the way we have learned is the acceptable way to treat people, particularly those who are different from us? What are some of the customary/cultural ways to see people?

1. People are creatures with their past still attached. So we don't reach out in forgiveness. Every one of us has skeletons in his closet. Someone has observed that there is so much good in the worst of us, and so much bad in the best of us, that it hardly behooves any one of us to talk about the rest of us. People around us need to see God's forgiveness with our skin wrapped around it. Perhaps one of the reasons people do not become Christians is because they cannot perceive that God is able to forgive as they watch Christians withhold forgiveness so often.

2. Another customary way to see people is to see them as creatures who are not to be trusted. We have learned in our lifetime not to trust other people, so we keep them at a distance. We hold off the newcomers. We do not openly share well with one another.

3. Another customary way to see people is to see them as creatures to recognize only. So we keep our relationships at the recognition level. We say, "Hi, how are you?" Twenty years later, we still have never said anything deeper than, "Hi, how are you?" And we never slow down enough to hear how they are, anyway. Are they hurting? Are they aching? Are they broken? We have become goaholics. We are on the go so much that we fail to notice the people around us.

4. Another customary way to see people is to see them outwardly only. So we size people up quickly by the externals. Is their hair too long? Do they listen to the wrong kind of music? Do they ever smoke, wear makeup, wear a beard? We judge each other too much by the external, circumstantial evidences, and then we make our verdicts.

I will never forget the first time I saw him. He had just entered the room of the "New Members Lab" at our church. When I first saw him from behind, I didn't know whether he was a he or a she. The hair was long in the back, and done in a ponytail. His name was Tim. I thought to myself at first, "What kind of person is this? He has a long beard and his hair is in a ponytail. He is not dressed neatly and walks with a limp." But during the introductory time, when each person told about himself, I began to see Tim differently. Tim had recently been a member of a very radical motorcycle gang in southern California. One of his buddies had been in a serious accident and was in the hospital, evidently dying. Tim was not a religious person, but he prayed to God that if God would let his buddy live, Tim would consider the possibility of looking into Jesus seriously.

Notice the promise was just to "consider the possibility." Well, the buddy lived through the accident. And Tim and his wife decided to take one step toward carrying out the promise. They attended our church one Sunday morning as visitors. When our preacher finished the sermon and gave the invitation, Tim started to walk out of the pew. His wife said, "Where are you going, Tim?" And Tim replied, "I'm going to take that Jesus he has been talking about as my Lord." That happened just two weeks earlier, and already Tim had led two of the other motorcycle gang members to the Lord. By three weeks later, he had been used by God to convert the hit man of that motorcycle gang. And he still had his ponytail and beard.

We are really the losers when we see people like trees and treat them as such.

There are other ways that we see and treat people like trees.

1. If we use them to our advantage and select only the best for our church, we see them like trees. The better trees we mark for cutting, and the other ones we just leave behind.

2. If we see them only as providers for various services, we see them like trees—good for shelter, shade, and lumber.

3. If we know of some in the area who seem strange, are alienated, and need kinship, but we go our way, we see them like trees that we can pass along the highway each day with little notice or care. When those trees fall, we really do not miss them!

4. If we know of some who have insufficient clothes or food, and we say, "The government will provide," we see them like forests that will be maintained by the interior department.

Jesus touched that blind man and he saw people like trees. Jesus knew that if that's the way he saw, he would be good for nothing in life. So Jesus touched him the second time.

Then he "began to see everything clearly" (Mark 8:25). He saw everything clearly because he saw people correctly. There is a real

95

sense in which we see nothing clearly until we see people in the way God sees people.

This was indeed a unique miracle done by Jesus. It is the only miracle that did not happen suddenly and instantaneously. The sight of that man returned gradually. Was this because Jesus had lost some of His power, used an incompetent method, or just didn't have the right touch at that particular moment? Of course not! Jesus was teaching us a significant lesson by the gradual returning of this man's vision. In that gradually developing sight, I think Jesus was teaching us that a person may not see people the way God wants him to see them the moment he becomes a disciple of Jesus. Sometimes we hear people teach and preach as if the moment a person becomes a Christian, he is instantaneously such a full-grown Christian that he will have no more problems with life. But that is not true!

However, in this miracle, Jesus made it clear that He wants us to develop a clear perception of people. He does not expect us to continue to wear our cultural blinders.

Many of us need that second touch from Jesus. Not a second experience with salvation, but a touch that comes because we now understand clearly how Jesus himself wants to see people through our eyes and touch them through our hands.

The ministry of the church, and thus the ministry of the members, cannot be determined by our savings account, but rather by our seeing account.

Can you begin to imagine what it would do for the church and to any community when God's people begin to see men correctly—as people created by God, who have sinned, who have feelings, who have hopes, and who deserve to be touched by God's people correctly? To see clearly will change our conduct. To see clearly will provide us with the kind of power to live abundantly the will of God.

Let us be open to be so filled by the Spirit of Christ that we will be willing instruments of uniting men to God with the love of God that flows through us. Let us beam a love to others that does not erase the differences that exist because of culture, group affiliations, race, or whatever, but will handle those differences because we are Christians. That all—just Christians—saying to the world of broken, alienated, estranged, and polarized people—our world in our time—this message: "God loves you. Christ loves you and gave himself for you. And I love you; so here I am!"

Let's let trees be trees and people be people, people with feelings and souls, who need forgiveness, companionship, trust, friendships—and our friendship. Let's let the surprisability of Jesus, who did this surprising miracle, continue to surprise people today. And it can if we are willing to surprise people with a surprising kind of sensitivity—because we see them correctly.

Let's determine to see people and treat people so differently that they can say to us—and mean it—something like this:

I love you not only for what you are, but for what I am when I am with you.

I love you for accepting me for who I am.

I love you for looking deeply into my life and seeing all the good that no one else looks long enough to find.

I love you for not highlighting all those weak things that you cannot help but notice.

I love you for not being a perfectionist and for not nitpicking all the ways that I do not live up to your expectations.

I love you for not seeing me with the cultural blinders that others have learned to wear.

I love you for helping me make out of the lumber of my life, not a tavern, but a temple.

I love you because you are you, and because He—Jesus—first loved us both.

I love you for letting the surprisability of Jesus surprise me through you.

I love you because you see me as *me* and not as a *tree*.

CHAPTER 9

The Second Look
Mark 8:27—9:1

Look Again

In the previous chapter, we saw a no-sighted man who needed a second touch. In this chapter, we will see nearsighted men who needed a second look. The blind man needed a second touch in order to see people correctly. Jesus' disciples needed a second look in order to see Jesus correctly. In fact, they would need more than this second look, because they continued to wear their blinders until after Jesus' resurrection.

It is not enough to see people correctly. We must also see Jesus correctly. In fact, our ability to see people correctly will be determined by our accuracy in seeing Jesus.

So after Jesus dealt with that blind man's outlook, He began to deal with the disciples' insight. He asked them this question, "Who do people say that I am?" (Mark 8:27).

Jesus did not ask this because He was a bit paranoid and wanted to check up on what was being said behind His back, as some of us might do from time to time. He wanted the disciples to examine whether or not their perspective of Jesus was determined more by the peer group than by himself. To allow other people to determine for the disciples what they thought of Jesus had many problems. Here are some of them:

1. A Restricted Religion. The people's perspective would have been too restrictive for the disciples, for the people had not had the privilege of walking, talking, and living with Jesus the way these disciples had. Consequently, the people's perspective at this time would have come more out of their own feelings than out of facts. Wouldn't it have been disappointing had the disciples allowed other people who had not spent time with Jesus to determine their insight about Jesus? But don't we do that sometimes today? Is it possible that we can spend much time looking closely at Jesus and then allow some people who have never spent any close-up time with Him to sway us in our position? Haven't we seen people who have spent years in Sunday School and been regular at worship services on Sunday mornings and Sunday evenings, and then at a very vulnerable time (perhaps during adolescence or when they enter college) allowed someone else to turn their faith against Jesus? Some person who has never read the Bible, attended church, or really known Jesus is allowed to explain Him away as a myth or a legend.

2. *A Hand-me-down Religion.* Any position we have about the Lord has started because someone else has shared his stance about Jesus with us. It may have been our parents, Sunday-school teachers, friends, or someone else. That's natural and as it should be, for God expects people to share with other people. But if our life commitment about Jesus is nothing more than mouthing what someone else has said, then we have nothing more than a second-hand religion. There comes a time when each one of us must let his heart catch up with his head. We must spend time with Jesus himself—in meditation, in prayer, in quietness, and in that inner wrestling. We must talk with Him—and listen. We must sense that we are walking with Him and He with us. We must have a very personal, intimate encounter with the person of Jesus, not just an intellectual exercise with the report about Jesus.

Had these disciples just mouthed what everyone else was saying as their own position, it would have been clear that they were not allowing their personal time with Jesus to be translated into a personal relationship.

3. *A Majority-vote Religion.* Jesus knew that the majority were not seeing Him as the Messiah. And Jesus knew the power of the majority vote. Would the disciples go with the majority? If so, they could have no influence in the world after the death and resurrection of Jesus, for it is God's will that the minority affect the majority. That's why the church has still not caught on to the fact that the majority are not to call the major shots in the church. We are so committed to democracy (and I do not want to be committed to any other form of government for a nation) that we are uncomfortable if democracy is not the rule in the church. But democracy is the rule of the people, and that is not to be the rule of the church. The church is to be a theocracy. God's church cannot move forward as He wants it to move if the crucial decisions in the church that can affect its growth are determined by the majority vote of people. Many of those people are newer Christians. In a highly mobile society, many will move on before

the decisions of that vote can be implemented. Many churches even wait to call their preaching minister until that person has been voted on by the entire congregation. Yet the entire congregation was not in on the various interviews that revealed the kind of personality, life-style, leadership abilities, and commitment of that candidate. Too many times an entire congregation will vote after hearing only one sermon. Surely it is wiser to allow the spiritual leaders of the church who have done the searching, the interviewing, the praying, and the sifting to call a man to the body out of their concern for the future of that body. And surely we must come to the place where we trust our leaders enough to allow that.

Just recently, I heard about a new church that was beginning in a large metropolitan area. The leaders of that nucleus had called a couple from 1500 miles away to be with them for several days. Intensive interviews took place. The small nucleus of leaders got to know this couple well. The preacher preached Sunday morning and his wife sang. The following week, all the people of the congregation voted. The majority wanted that couple to lead them, but twenty people did not vote at all because they said, "We are not sure what we want in a preacher." So the couple was not called.

How do newer Christians know what they want in a preacher? How do many people know what they want in a preacher? And isn't it true that what they "want" in a preacher may be precisely what God knows they do not need? The consumer mentality has captured us in the church. We look for what will benefit us most when we go to Sears and J. C. Penney. We want the most for the least. Few buy in the consumer world for how what they purchase will benefit others. Every time God's people voted in the Old Testament, the majority was wrong. Probably the fewer the items that the whole congregation votes on, the better the momentum of the growth may be.

4. *A Religion Based on Peer Pressure.* Peer pressure is real. Many have sacrificed principles for popularity. We all want to be liked and accepted. But Jesus needed to have it settled whether or not His disciples were going to go for popularity. If what the others said about Jesus would determine the disciples' confession, then it would surely determine their conduct. Jesus expected His men to stand up with something different from the rest of the crowd. Would they? Do we? A Gallup poll should not determine

for us either our confession or our conduct. If it does, we will go the way of the world. And the world without Christ is headed toward Hell.

The disciples answered Jesus' question (verse 28). Their answers showed that they were indeed aware of what people around them were saying. They did not live a life of isolation from others because they were on the inside with Jesus. They knew how to relate to and talk with people. They knew the trends. They knew the thoughts. They knew the feelings of others. They were disciples of Jesus, but they were also involved in the world. And that's the way Jesus wants His disciples to be. In fact, on the night He was betrayed, He prayed that His disciples would not be taken out of the world (John 17:15). Light cannot affect darkness if it is put under a bucket. Salt and leaven cannot affect their environment if they are kept in shakers and boxes.

I know some people who, since becoming Christians, have become dropouts from the world. They have quit taking the newspaper and quit listening to news on television and radio because they do not want to know all of the junk that is going on in the world.

Jesus' apostles were not like that. They knew what others were saying about Jesus, and they told Him, "John the Baptist; and others say Elijah; but others, one of the prophets." None of those ways of seeing Jesus was a mean way. None of those ways was intended to malign Jesus. John the Baptist was a crowd mover. His preaching made a difference. Elijah had the courage to stand alone and had prayer power with God as few other men had. The prophets were inspired by God. But every one of those descriptions of Jesus could have started a cult. Those cults today that give Christianity the toughest times are led by people who claim great things for Jesus—"He is a good man; He was inspired; He was a prophet." But any description of Jesus that is less than the fact that He is the promised Messiah and thus is the *only* way to God is totally unacceptable to the Father.

Any human Christian leader today would love to be identified as a modern-day John the Baptist, Elijah, or other prophet. In fact, some are so interested in those designations that they claim that they are one of the prophets. But Jesus is not satisfied with any of those descriptions, for He was not merely human. He was God in flesh. And to whittle God down to the level of the greatest human being is heresy.

So Jesus continued to question the disciples (Mark 8:29). He wanted to know whether they stood with or against their fellow human beings, "Who do *you* say that I am?"

Peter went right to the heart of it, "Thou art the Christ." But what does that mean?

The word *Christ* is a title, not a name. We talk a lot about Jesus Christ. Jesus is the name; Christ is His title. It is like President Reagan. Reagan is the name; President is the title. The title stresses intentional function. And there is as much emphasis on *intention* as the function. It is not function done by accident. It is not a side issue. It is not a hobby. It is the priority issue in a man's life. While the Greek word is *Christ*, the Hebrew word is *Messiah*. It refers to God's anointed One. This is the one and only one that God has been planning for and prophesied about.

In order to understand better what God's unique anointed One would do in His intentional function, God anointed some forerunners in the Old Testament. He anointed prophets, priests, and kings. All three of these were combined in Jesus. As the prophet, He gives us God's message without fail. In fact, He made it clear that He does not speak on His own initiative, "but the Father Himself who sent Me has given Me commandment, what to say, and what to speak" (John 12:49).

As the priest, He obtains forgiveness for us by the sacrifice He offered. The disciples had a tough time with that, as we will see in a moment. Jesus made it clear that He came "to give His life a ransom for many" (Matthew 20:28).

As the king, He has *all* authority and power on earth. He made it clear, "All authority has been given to Me in heaven and on earth" (Matthew 28:18).

Is it enough just to confess that Jesus is the Christ? Of course not! It is not enough to say that if we only name Him with our lips that we can claim Him with our lives. Some people seem to think that they have secured Jesus for themselves just because they have defined Him as the Christ, the Son of the living God. But Jesus himself made it clear that not everyone who names Him clearly knows Him correctly, "Not everyone who says to Me, 'Lord, Lord,' will enter the kingdom of heaven; but he who does the will of My Father who is in heaven" (Matthew 7:21).

It was easy for Peter to say that Jesus was the Christ in a crowd of eleven others who all believed it. But it was not that easy for Peter later in the courtyard when he was asked if he knew Jesus.

Then Peter not only refused to admit that Jesus was the Christ, but refused to claim that he even knew anyone with the name of Jesus.

Jesus' reply to Peter is shocking; it's unbelievable. "He warned them to tell no one about Him." (Mark 8:30). Jesus was saying, "If that's all you can say about me, then be still. You don't yet have enough to say. Your understanding is too narrow. Just shut up for a while."

You see, up to this time the disciples had seen Jesus in His authority and power. He had demonstrated His power over nature, His power over sin, His power over disease, and His power over the death of another one. They liked the idea of Jesus' living with authority and power. As a matter of fact, that's precisely how all Judaism had been anticipating the coming of the Messiah.

The Jewish faith had linked only those prophecies that dealt with power and expansion to the coming of their Messiah, such as this one from Isaiah:

> For a child will be born to us, a son will be given to us;
> And the government will rest on His shoulders;
> And His name will be called Wonderful Counselor, Mighty God,
> Eternal Father, Prince of Peace.
> There will be no end to the increase of His government or of peace,
> On the throne of David and over his kingdom,
> To establish it and to uphold it with justice and righteousness
> From then on and forevermore"   (Isaiah 9:6, 7).

The Jewish people were tired of being a political football, kicked back and forth by every kind of foreign occupation. And they remembered the time of David and Solomon, who expanded the Jewish kingdom across the geography to its greatest amount of territory. During those days, all kinds of people were under the rule of the Jewish king. But since that time, the kingdom had fallen apart, been split up, been absorbed by others, and had been mistreated, occupied, and reduced to a very small geographical area that was held by occupational troops.

So they looked at those prophecies that talked about a time when someone would come and re-establish the government, increase it, sit upon a throne, and establish that kingdom forever and ever. That made them think about a Messiah who would establish an earthly kingdom and would manifest significant un-challenging, unsurpassed, and never-to-be-defeated political power on earth.

The Jewish leaders yearned for that time when they would be in control of the Egyptians, the Syrians, the Romans, and the Greeks. That's the kind of Messiah they prayed for. That's the kind of Messiah they wanted. And if we had lived with them in those days under their oppression, that's the kind of hope we, too, would have kept burning in our hearts. You can only lose so many battles before you look for a new general. You can only lose so many games before you yearn for a new coach.

Between the Old and New Testament writings were days in which this kind of Messianic hope escalated within the Jewish nation. During this time, Jewish writers wrote many pieces of literature that connected the promised Messiah to their power needs. They cranked up in their writings the hopes that the Messiah would do the following:

1. Gather all the scattered Jews into one place again.
2. Rebuild Jerusalem to be the greatest city in the world.
3. Subdue all political oppositions and hostile people.
4. Re-establish worldwide peace and goodness forever, because all the rest of the world would be under the rule of Judaism.
5. That rule would never end on earth.

Consequently, Jewish leaders taught that when the Messiah did come, He would never die. They overlooked some of the most significant prophecies about the Messiah, such as Isaiah 53 (which talks about the Messiah's being smitten, oppressed, afflicted, and cut off from the land of the living in death). After all, who wants a Messiah who is going to be killed by the very people you want to conquer?

So if all that Jesus' disciples were going to say is that He is the Messiah, then that statement (left all by itself) would have misled the Jewish people and been misunderstood by the Greeks. There has to be more—and there is!

Jesus began to teach them that their understanding of the living Christ must be balanced with their understanding of the dying Christ. "And He began to teach them that the Son of Man must suffer many things and be rejected by the elders and the chief

105

priests and the scribes, and be killed, and after three days rise again" (Mark 8:31). Jesus was giving them the second look at himself. They had seen Him in the abundant life; now they had to see Him in an agonizing death. They had seen Him in power; now they had to be willing to see Him in what appeared to be weakness. They had seen Him in popularity; now they had to see Him in shame.

But Peter rebuked Jesus. Peter allowed his prior understanding of the Messiah to continue to be the blinders he wore, that affected his look. Peter and the other disciples knew very well the understanding of the Jewish people, "We have heard out of the Law that the Christ is to remain forever; and how can You say, 'The Son of Man must be lifted up'?" (John 12:34).

Is Peter's response really too difficult to understand? Who among us wants our hopes to die? If we were members of a glorious growing church that began to fall apart, split apart, and dwindle, wouldn't we look for a dynamic new leader who could bring us to renewal and growth? Who would want that leader to die in three years? That wouldn't be enough time to know all the members well, let alone the community. That would not be enough time to understand the problems that had brought decay to that once glorious church. Surely we can understand Peter's response. Peter's response zeroed in on the words, "be killed," but not on the words, "after three days rise again."

Peter's response to Jesus also indicated that at this time he failed to submit to the authority of the Messiah. If Jesus is the Christ—the Messiah—then what He says is authoritative. And no one who confesses that He is the Christ should take any other position than to be totally submitted to whatever He says. But as soon as Peter confessed that Jesus was the Christ, he began to argue with the Christ and claim that he himself had some insight that the Christ did not have.

The moment we name Jesus as the Christ of our lives is the moment we should give up the right to say anything but an immediate amen to what Jesus says. But do we? If we think we do, then let's see how well we handle what Jesus went on to say.

Don't Just Wear the Cross—Bear It

Jesus responded to Peter's rebuke with a rebuke, "Get behind Me, Satan; for you are not setting your mind on God's interests, but man's" (Mark 8:33).

106

Satan had been trying since Jesus' birth to detour Him from going to the cross. For until someone who has never sinned dies on the cross for everyone else's sins, then Satan has all sinners with him in Hell. But if someone dies not just physically, but also is separated from the Father for a time for man's sins, then man can be forgiven in that person's sacrifice. Satan knew that. He also knew that all of those who commit to the Savior immediately become deserters from Satan's side. From the birth of Jesus, Satan had been trying to block Jesus.

And now Satan tried again through the heart of one of Jesus' own disciples. Peter was a friend of Jesus. Peter was one of the three with whom Jesus spent most of His time. It is not unheard of for Satan to work through the voice of a close friend in trying to detour us from the right path. Sometimes those who are the closest to us with the best intentions try to change our directions. Perhaps the most deceiving and yet most persuasive approach of the devil is to seek to influence us through the voice of those whom we love the most and whom we know really seek our good. Satan had tried to detour Jesus through His enemies, His family, religious leaders, and now through one of Jesus' close friends.

Notice that Peter did not rebuke Jesus in front of the others. He took Jesus aside. It must have been a tender moment for the two. It was surely a sincere moment for Peter. Peter's rebuke toward Jesus probably came in the package of compassion, tenderness, pleading, begging, and personal request with hurt. But even the pleading love and the pleading voice of intimate love and friendship did not deter Jesus from carrying on the will of God—even though His humanness did not want to be nailed to the cross. Isn't it a powerful influence when the loving voice of a close friend is counseling you not to do something that you yourself know you will not enjoy? That's what Jesus faced on this day. But He knew that the will of God was more significant for the well-being of mankind than the wishes of His close friends. Each one of us must remember this episode in Jesus' life and follow His example when we have the same influence tugging at our hearts to go a different route than what we sense is God's will for our lives—even when those closest to us beg us with tears, warmth, and intimacy.

Up to this time, the disciples had been following Jesus' popularity, following Jesus' power, following Jesus' miracles, and following Jesus' authority. They were content in that. They felt privileged in that. They were indeed special in that.

But here Jesus was talking about a different kind of following, "If anyone wishes to come after Me, let him deny himself, and take up his cross, and follow Me" (Mark 8:34).

When Jesus said a disciple must "deny himself," He was not saying that we have to hate ourselves. There is too much self hate going on in the world already. In fact, Jesus makes it clear that we are to love others as we love ourselves (Matthew 22:39).

To love ourselves does not mean we love selfishness. It means that we recognize that we have worth in the eyes of God. We mean something. We are worth something. We have value. We are unique and different. We don't have to be like someone else.

If to deny self does not mean to hate self, then what does it mean? It means to be willing to say no to the greedy, grasping self. We must be willing to say no to the temptation of hoarding materials for self only instead of being willing to use them for others. We must be willing to say no when we are tempted to do the fun things that from God's perspective are forbidden things. We must be willing to say no when we are tempted to put down others, criticize them, and hinder them from progress in the program. We must be willing to say no when we are asked to believe that any other Christian in any other group is a non-Christian and thus not worthy of fellowship, recognition, and a sense of unity.

We must be willing to say no when we are tempted to come down from the cross. To deny oneself really means to "take up his cross." But what does it mean to take up the cross? It does not mean just to wear it as jewelry, as many people do today, but it means to bear it. It doesn't mean to wear it on clothes, but to bear it in conduct.

To take up the cross means, at the very minimum, that we are willing to die to selfishness and live for God. It means, at the very minimum, that we take into our lives what we witness Jesus did on the cross.

1. To take up our cross is to set a goal for our lives. Jesus set a goal for His life and did not detour from it. He set His face toward the cross. Too many times, we are wishy-washy. We don't settle on our life goals. So we get tossed to and fro with every bit of fad and wind that blows.

2. To take up our cross is to not let our inner feelings have the final word. Jesus did not let His inner feelings have the final word. In the Garden of Gethsemane, His inner feelings kept saying, "I don't want to go through this tomorrow. It will hurt; it will be shameful; it will be lonely. My individual will wants to say no." Jesus did not let His feelings have the final say. His commitment was, "Not My will, but Thine be done" (Luke 22:42).

3. To take up our cross is to not defend ourselves. Jesus did not defend himself. He could have called down multitudes of angels and defended himself prior to going to that cross (Matthew 26:53). But He refused to do so. Those people were surely fortunate that it was Jesus on that day and not I. If I had Jesus' power, I would not have called multitudes of angels together, but I would have created out of nothing about sixteen Sherman tanks, a dozen jet planes, and a hundred bazookas and let them have it. You see, no one in that day had ever seen a tank or a plane or a bazooka. I would have done something on that day that the world would never have forgotten.

Jesus did do something on that day that the world has never forgotten. He refused to defend himself. And the world has not gotten over that yet. He didn't blame others. He didn't tell them how wrong they were. He didn't demand status. He didn't demand to be treated in accordance with His credentials. In fact, He came riding into Jerusalem on the back of a colt instead of a white horse, as status-seeking people would have done.

4. To take up our cross is to forgive. Jesus said, "Father, forgive them" (Luke 23:34). It is easy for us to forgive those who hurt us by mistake. Many times that happens. People are not always aware that they are offending us or paining us. When they say, "I'm sorry, I certainly didn't mean that," we are easily motivated to forgive. But what if someone hurts us on purpose? What if they have planned for a long time to do us in? What if they persuaded and manipulated others to join them in taking us down, hurting us, maligning us, or destroying us? That's what happened to Jesus on the cross. It was not an oversight. It was not an accident. It was schemed. It was planned. It was deceitful. It was intentional. And the people who did it loved every moment of it.

But it was of those people that Jesus said, "Father, forgive them."

5. To take up our cross is to be willing to be identified with the untouchables. Jesus was. He was crucified between two thieves and made it clear that one of those would spend eternity in fellowship with Him. To take up our cross and follow Him is to be willing to spend time with the dying people around us, those with whom other religious folks will have no dealings. Let's not forget that we are all physically dying. If the dying ones around us are to have eternal life, we must be willing to spend time with them—even if it is painful time. Jesus' time on the cross with those thieves was indeed painful.

What is the major hindrance to taking up our cross and following Jesus and the cross-bearing kind of life? It is that we do not want to be inconvenienced. So Jesus addressed that, too: "For whoever wishes to save his life shall lose it; but whoever loses his life for My sake and the gospel's shall save it" (Mark 8:35). There He was contrasting selfless living with selfish living. He was talking about setting goals that go beyond our own self-interest for the benefit of others. It is only when we do so that we really become a whole individual. Every person remains a psychological adolescent until he makes a decision for a cause outside of himself, one that is bigger than he and will benefit others even at the cost of personal benefit.

What hinders us from giving up self for others? Jesus went on to explain that hindrance: we are tempted to store up for self rather than serve out for others. "For what does it profit a man to gain the whole world, and forfeit his soul?" (Mark 8:36). To store up in the world for self instead of using what we have for others is to store up that which is eventually going to be destroyed. Everything we store up is potential junk; so we end up saving what we cannot keep and sacrificing what we should not lose.

This response by Jesus really communicates to us our significant worth. Let's pretend you have just won the sweepstake prize on a major television game show. In front of you are two curtains. You can choose all the prizes behind either one. Curtain number one opens, and behind it are these prizes:

a. A round-the-world trip for four people for three months with all expenses paid—travel, lodging, meals, tips, and all, plus $50,000 cash for buying souvenirs.

b. New his and her Mercedes automobiles with a new replacement every two years for the rest of your life.

c. A new house worth $350,000 to be built on any site you choose, plus $120,000 for the purpose of buying the site.

d. An active oil well that is producing 1000 barrels a day. All expenses for keeping the well active will be paid with all royalties to be given to you.

e. An all-expense four-year scholarship for a college education at the college of your choice for two of your children or grandchildren.

f. A $3,000,000 certificate to be invested so that it will pay you $300,000 a year for the rest of your life. Upon your death, the certificate will be given to your survivors.

That's behind curtain number one, and you may choose all of that as your grand prize, or you can choose what is behind curtain number two. So curtain number two opens. It looks barren except for one object in the middle of the stage, a rather unkempt, staggering Hispanic who is obviously under the influence of alcohol. And that's all there is behind curtain number two.

Now make your choice! Which curtain would you choose? Well, behind which curtain is the most value? Take that unkempt Hispanic who is under the influence of alcohol away, and replace him with one of your children. Now behind which curtain is the most value? Take your child away and put yourself behind curtain number two. Now behind which curtain is the most value? It does not really make any difference which person is behind curtain number two. The person behind curtain number two is worth far more value than everything behind curtain number one. That's what Jesus was getting at when He said, "What does it profit a man to gain the whole world, and forfeit his soul?" A person who does that has been duped by the greatest and oldest con game in history. We have been duped into believing that things are more important than people, and it is precisely that philosophy that prevents us from taking Jesus' cross and following Him in a cross-bearing kind of life-style.

Whatever you continue to pile up behind curtain number one, you can't pile up enough. That's what Jesus meant when He said, "For what shall a man give in exchange for his soul?" There is no equal price. Who in the world would give a ten-karat perfect diamond or a one-ton brick of solid gold for a dandelion? The diamonds and the gold are long lasting, but the dandelion is so temporary. It is here today and gone tomorrow. But that is precisely the kind of comparison Jesus was getting at with those disciples. When we prize things and possessions, we are prizing the temporary. Of course, we may make those our priorities for fifty, sixty, seventy, or eighty years, but how long is that time compared to eternity? Go outside now and look into the sky. Draw a line from one end of the horizon to the other. Then put one little dot in the middle of that line. That little dot represents the time span on planet earth while the line across the sky begins to represent the time span of eternity.

To be ashamed of Jesus now is to lose Him in eternity (Mark 8:38). To be ashamed of Jesus now is to refuse to serve man as He did. A soldier today cannot become a deserter and expect to receive the "Medal of Honor." A college student cannot drop out and expect to graduate. Married couples cannot turn their backs on each other and expect to celebrate their fiftieth wedding anniversary. And we cannot cop out on Jesus during our lives and expect Him to be proud of us when He comes back.

Jesus has made it clear He is coming back. "When He comes in the glory of His Father with the holy angels . . ." (Mark 8:38).

But that promise of His return did not give His disciples a reason to sit around and do nothing while they waited for Him to return. Jesus' kingdom was going to come in their lifetime, with power (Mark 9:1). Jesus promised that people would not taste death in that day before they saw His kingdom come with power. And they did indeed see His kingdom come with power. His *kingdom* refers to His rule, His reign, His authority, and His territory. That kingdom came with power on the day of Pentecost and spread throughout the whole known world. From twelve to a multitude that no man could count, from Palestine (which was only 120 miles long and 40 miles wide) to the entire geographical population of the world, and from one race to all categories of people—that's the kingdom and the power with which it came.

From Jesus' defeat on the cross came victory. From His burial came blessings. From the cross came the crown. And so it is today.

Jesus calls us to both privilege and purpose. He has not dangled out in front of us just the rewards and niceties. He has let us know immediately that His invitation to us is not just to be "saved," but also to begin serving. That's what our confession of Christ is all about—both salvation and service. That's what baptism is all about. It is a burial of selfishness followed by a resurrection to a newness of life.

Jesus never diluted His invitation to an invitation for people to come just for what they could get out of it—forgiveness, salvation, Heaven—but also for what they could give out of it.

That's what Jesus means when His invitation is, "Come and follow Me." That's the "second look."

CHAPTER 10

Help My Unbelief
Mark 9:14-29

Mark 9:14-29 records a miracle that Matthew and Luke also included. However, Mark recorded some details of this miracle that are found in no other Gospel. Only Mark recorded most of the details from verses 21 through 29.

Those details left volumes of holes and yet gave significant challenge to the Christians in Rome who were going through difficult times. And they speak significantly to us today.

All three Synoptic Gospel writers record this miracle as happening immediately after Jesus came down from the mountaintop with Peter, James, and John.

Many of us ought to get away from the crowds from time to time in a sort of mountaintop retreat, as did Jesus with those three apostles. Those kind of getaways can give us time for quietness, meditation, prayer, feeding upon the Word, and making commitments.

But we cannot stay on the mountaintop forever. Following time on the mountain, we must come down into the valley where the crowds are—where the freeways are jammed with five-mile-per-hour traffic, where the air is polluted with smog, where there is honking, shoving, pushing, and yelling, where the quietness is replaced with noise and slowness by haste, where peace touches perplexity, where prayer touches problems, where the Word touches the world.

Getting away is important! Some people are such rushaholics, goaholics, and workaholics that they feel guilty in a spiritual getaway.

There were times when Jesus had to order His apostles to do that, "Come away by yourselves to a lonely place and rest a while" (Mark 6:31). That was Jesus' way of saying, "Come apart—lest you come apart."

But getting away from the world does not give us permission to stay away from the world when we come down from the

113

mountain. A retreat is to help better us to advance into the world with the mind-set of Christ, not remove from the world with the mind-set of cowards. Time away is meant to equip us better to cope with the nitty-gritty and humdrum on one hand, and for the stressful demands of everyday life on the other. So as soon as the four came down from that mountain, Jesus led them to the crowds where there were needs. Immediately, they saw the crowd gathered around the other disciples. Mark records something the other Gospel writers did not—the crowds were arguing with those other disciples.

What was the crowd arguing about with those disciples? The text does not plainly tell us, but the context does. The crowd was arguing with the disciples about the seeming lack of power those disciples had to heal this boy.

The disciples had tried to do a miracle and it did not work. The crowd was arguing with them concerning their impotence. Can't you hear them say that if Jesus was indeed the Messiah—God in flesh, then the disciples would have been able to have pulled off this power-miracle?

The Christians in Rome needed to hear that because, no doubt, many in Rome had been throwing the same kind of argument against those Christians. "If your God were really that all-powerful God who loves you and protects you, then you would not be going through these kinds of persecutions. He would deliver you from them. You must be doing something to anger your God to be getting this kind of treatment." Let's face it, most of us from time to time have asked those same kinds of questions when the situations got tough for us.

Jesus asked the people to bring the boy to Him. What an amazing involvement of Jesus. He had just finished talking about going to the cross and had just been on a mountain retreat. But neither one of those prevented Jesus from facing the crisis of the moment.

It would have been easy for Jesus to have talked about the cross in the future and bypassed the calamities of peoples' lives in the present. Isn't it easy for us to do that? Sometimes we think that all we should do is minister to peoples' spiritual needs, but not get involved in the temporary, physical, human pains of this world.

But Jesus never thought like that! He knew that His Father had created the whole person—not just that part of the person that is eternal. So Jesus cared for the whole man and woman. Jesus saw

114

what was going on with that boy (Mark 9:20). He knew how long he had suffered (Mark 9:21). And Jesus had compassion. The father of the son came to the disciples and to Jesus with some mixed feelings. The very fact that he brought his son to Jesus indicates a measure of faith. Probably the inner man in him believed that Jesus could do it, but no doubt his intellectual rationality had a tough time believing it. So he said to Jesus, "If You can do anything, take pity on us and help us!" (Mark 9:22). Using the word *if* shows reluctance. Even his request shows some reluctance. He did not say, "Heal my son," for he had evidently asked the disciples to cure the son (Mark 9:18), but that did not work. So he weakened his request a bit from curing the son to just "help us."

While the man had been putting the responsibility on Jesus by saying, "If you can do anything," Jesus threw the comment back to the man with a challenging responsibility, "If *you* can! All things are possible to him who believes" (Mark 9:23[1]).

When Jesus said, "If *you* can," He was making it clear that the issue did not lie in Jesus' ability, but in that man's willingness to set no limits on what can be accomplished through the power of God. When Jesus said, "All things are possible to him who believes," He was making it clear that by faith we unleash and participate in the sovereign power of God.

Do we really believe that today? I used to say that the issue between an active God in Bible days and a passive God that I had accepted for today was not that God had less power, but that God put limits on the use of His power today. Certainly God does limit how He manifests His power as any benevolent person does. But I used to claim to know exactly where all those limits were. I had God in my hip pocket. I had God in a little box. I knew what He could and couldn't do and was uncomfortable if anyone else considered God to be bigger than the God I had.

Is our God too small for the twentieth century—the century of computers and cancer, the century of the escalation of abortion,

---

[1]Note the words quoted from Mark 9:23 are from the New American Standard Bible. The punctuation, however, is the author's. Since the Greek manuscripts included no punctuation, the punctuation in English Bibles represents the translators' *interpretation,* and in this case, the author has interpreted the passage differently.

child abuse, homosexuality, bankruptcy, and pornography? Is God too small for the rise of teenage suicide, AIDS, abortions, unwed mothers, and drug abuse? Is God too small for our pressure-cooker schedules and for mid-life crises? Is God too small for our rapidly growing mass urban areas? Today, twenty percent of the population of the United States now lives in ten cities, and in the next fifteen years, more people will live in world cities with populations of more than 100,000 than was the entire population of the world in 1960.

Is God too small for the 17,000 different people groups that are completely untouched with the Gospel? Is God too small for those spiritual principalities and powers of darkness that are invading planet earth and taking man's mind captive to obey Satan?

Is God too small for all of that?

Or is it possible that our thinking about God is too small? I read a plaque recently that said, "Think small. Big ideas upset everyone." In the religious world, we have also said, "Believe small. Big faith upsets people." But it may be that we are upsetting too few people today with our faith in the bigness of God.

Just how big is our God today—a big, adequate, almighty God for the first century with its slow sailboats, dusty roads, candlelight, donkeys, swords, sandals, water drawn out of wells, and bread made by hand? Sure, of course! God is big enough for all of that antiquity way back then!

But how about in the 1980s with our Ph.D.'s, J.D.'s, Th.D.'s, M.D.'s, and all the other little D's? Do we really need an active, almighty, supra-natural God when we have heart transplants, supermarkets, insurance companies, medical clinics, *Tylenol,* laser surgery, call-waiting telephones, satellites, labeled jeans, stereos, cars, moonwalks, and Disneyland?

Do we need the God-u-factured as long as we ourselves are so powerful and satisfied with so much of the manufactured?

I want to be confessional and repentant at this point. I have spent too much of my time cutting God down to the size of man. In fact, to less than man's size. For I have not been willing to give God credit for the unbelievable. But name it, and I have believed that with enough time, man would someday do it. So we praise man's potential and explain away God's power for the modern age. We fantasize about man's explosive ability for the twenty-first century, and we freeze God's extraordinary activity back to the first century.

We have put God in a box. We have Him trapped in our boxes of theology, outlines, formulas, schemes, and unwritten creeds. But our boxes are too small for the God of this universe. His thoughts and His ways are still as far above ours as the heavens are above the earth. And He has not stopped thinking, nor has He stopped acting.

I cannot believe that God is happy with us when we intentionally and intellectually whittle Him down to a wimp who has left all of His miraculous power confined to the pages of past history.

God is not just the Lord of the first century. He is also the Lord of every century. He is not just the Lord of the first creation. He is also the Lord of the new creation. He is not just the Lord of the exodus back then. He is also the Lord of the environment right now. He is not just the Lord of Heaven up there. He is also the Lord of earth down here.

The confession of Jeremiah must again become the confession of God's people, "Ah Lord God! Behold, Thou hast made the heavens and the earth by Thy great power and by Thine outstretched arm! Nothing is too difficult for Thee" (Jeremiah 32:17).

If life is bigger than we are—and it is—then we need a God who is bigger than we to help us through it. If God is not bigger, or is not able or not willing to help, or has restricted himself to passivity, then we might just as well hold a pity party for ourselves. Is that one reason there is so much depression, discouragement, and ambivalence in today's world?

Let's lift up the bigness of God in our singing, in our worship, in our testimonies, in our talk, in our expectations, in our giving, in our living, and in our life-style.

And let's lift up the bigness of God in our prayers. Let's be willing to ask God for miraculous healings, miraculous restoration of broken relationships, for divine intervention, and for changes in our daily life-styles.

Let's admit that we have some unbeliefs. Let's admit that we have boxes in which we have God trapped. And then ask God to help us open those boxes and let Him out.

While at one time I had God in a box and claimed to know the limits of how He would operate in any situation, today, here is my answer for knowing the limits of God:

1. Nothing is too difficult for God.
2. His ways and His thoughts are still higher than ours.

3. He is the same yesterday, today, and forever.
4. He can do whatever He wants to do.
5. All things are possible with God.

That father responded well to Jesus' insistence that some of the responsibility lay on his own belief system. He became humble. He became little. He became honest. He became transparent. He became confessional. For he said, "I do believe; help my unbelief."

That father was admitting, "I have set limits on God. Within those limits is my belief. Beyond those limits is my unbelief. I have put God inside my little box. But instead of God's being trapped inside of it, I am trapped inside of it. Help me, Jesus."

You see, Jesus had just said that this is an unbelieving generation (Mark 9:19). And that man was confessing, "I know it. I am a part of that unbelieving generation. My belief goes so far, and then unbelief sets in. O God, set me free!"

Most of us know about that. Most of us have allowed our educational, intellectual, scientific world of observation and cause and effect to belittle the God of power. Most of us need to humble ourselves and honestly say to God, "Help my unbelief. Fill me with awe. Fill me with respect. Fill me with worship. Fill me with the Holy Spirit. Fill me with expectations. Fill me with a faith that God *is* able—not just *was* able, and not just *will be* able—but God *is able now*. Help my unbelief."

But that's risky. It means we may take a faith stance that others around us have not been accustomed to. It means we are willing to go out on a limb in our prayers and in our expectations. But those who receive the fruit are willing to go out on a limb for God. Let us not be a people who continue to fulfill 2 Timothy 3:5, a people "holding to a form of godliness, although they have denied its power." Jesus did not stay buried. The Holy Spirit did not give up the ghost at the end of the first century. God is neither dead nor impotent. He is still doing the unbelievable.

Jesus did not say, "All things are possible only in the first century to him who believes." Nor did Jesus say, "All things are possible only to the apostles." Nor did Jesus say, "All things are possible only to those upon whom the apostles have laid their hands." No! Jesus said, "All things are possible to him who believes." And where the Bible speaks, let us also speak.

What a message for those Christians in Rome, who were under such oppression that it appeared that they and their God were impotent. Christians throughout the centuries who have been in difficult times have realized tremendous growth when they have lifted their hearts, heads, hands, and spirits to the almighty power of God and believed in Him.

After Jesus healed the boy, the apostles asked Jesus why they could not do it. Jesus replied, "This kind cannot come out by anything but prayer." Some manuscripts also include, "and fasting." Evidently the apostles had been doing powerful things in the name of Jesus without putting those activities in prayer. Isn't it easy to just go ahead and work something when it has worked without spending much time in prayer? Jesus was reminding those apostles that God's work was not done just by the natural means of human ingenuity and availability. Even though those apostles had been living close to Jesus, they needed to pray. What a lesson for all of us!

Regardless of how much time, energy, and sacrifice we spend doing the Lord's work, studying His Word, and meditating in the presence of Jesus, we need to maintain close verbal contact with God to be the kind of people through whom God can work in extraordinary ways. If we don't, we will not only lose our vitality, but also our humility, because we will begin to think that anything that happens is because of our own doing.

A weakened faith often accompanies prayerlessness. And prayerlessness results in powerlessness. This situation was aggravated by a weak faith on the part of the father and a weakened prayer life on the part of the apostles. No wonder that boy never got helped!

Does God still do the unexpected today? Of course He does!

A few years ago, I had just arrived in Kansas City to hold a meeting. Julia, my wife, called and said that she had just received a call from Marcella Linn. She told me that Marcella's husband, Don (they are close friends of ours), who was ministering in Indiana, was holding a revival in St. Joseph, Missouri, and he had just had an automobile accident. Julia related that Marcella wanted me to go to the hospital, but she didn't know any of the details. I went to the hospital and could not believe it when I looked at Don Linn. I did not recognize him. The doctors told me, "There is no way that he will live through the night. He has massive internal injuries." They had a tube in his side—blood was pouring out. He had already lost several pints of blood. The doctors said, "We have no idea of the problems inside, because there is too much blood, but he has a broken back." The doctors showed me on X ray how it was broken and the mess it was in. He said, "He cannot live through the night."

Marcella and people in the church flew out that night, and I picked them up at 1:00 A.M. That was Saturday. Sunday, the doctors said, "He's made it through the night, but he cannot make it through the day." Monday—on the critical list—"He cannot make it through the day!"

I called into the switchboard on Tuesday and said, "I would like to talk to Mrs. Don Linn. This was the operator who answers all incoming calls to the hospital, and she said, "Oh, you mean the wife of the preacher who is dying?" That's not the way to answer a hospital phone, but that's the way she answered it!

Wednesday morning, I called again to tell Marcella we were coming up that night. It was the Wednesday before Thanksgiving, and we were going to spend time with her. I called the floor that Don was on and asked the nurse if I could speak to Mrs. Don Linn.

The nurse said, "Well, she is not here right now, but Mr. Linn just walked by."

Well, I knew that she just didn't understand what was going on; so I said, "No, I don't want to talk to him. I want to talk with Mrs. Linn."

I got Marcella on the phone. She told me that on that morning, Don was in severe pain and they had hardly been able to move him because of that pain, but suddenly he said, "My pain is gone!" They could not believe it. He got up—no pain! He put his feet on the floor—no pain! He took a walk—no pain! He went to the X-ray room—no internal injuries—no broken back!

God is able!

I met her at a Christ in Youth Conference. She told me about her last pregnancy. On the fourth day of that pregnancy, she had had severe pain. She had never had pain in any of her other pregnancies. Two weeks later, it was discovered that the baby was in the fallopian tube. The mother went bedfast. Her husband carried her everywhere. They prayed, "God, don't let this baby die! We want this baby!" In the ninth week of that pregnancy, she could not do anything by herself. Her husband had not been to work for six weeks. He had to roll her over in the bed and carry her everywhere. The doctors said, "We are going to have to take the baby. If we don't, both the baby and the mother will die." The morning the surgery was scheduled, our sister awoke at 4:00 A.M., and there was no pain! She thought she had had a miscarriage. She looked around, and there was no evidence of that. She got out of bed very weak, but with no pain. She went downstairs—no pain! They took her to the doctor. The doctor discovered that the baby had miraculously moved from the fallopian tube and was now in perfect position in the womb. They brought in three specialists from the Mayo Clinic. They declared it a miracle. And that girl that was born is now eighteen years old.

God is able!

Surely God wants us to be a people who pray for big things because we believe in a big God. Surely God would be delighted that we be known as people whose prayer meetings are larger than our meetings for musical concerts.

We should be a people who believe that nothing is impossible. At the same time, we must stick with Habakkuk:

> Though the fig tree should not blossom,
> And there be no fruit on the vines,
> Though the yield of the olive should fail,
> And the fields produce no food,
> Though the flock should be cut off from the fold,
> And there be no cattle in the stalls,
> Yet I will exult in the Lord,
> I will rejoice in the God of my salvation.
> The Lord God is my strength,
> And He has made my feet like hinds' feet,
> And makes me walk on my high places (Habakkuk 3:17-19).

That means we ask believing that God knows so much more than all of us together. That means that even if Don Linn had died, and if that baby in the mother had died, we will believe in God and will exult in Him and know that He is on our side. The cross and the resurrection prove it!

God wants to see us be a people whose worship services are celebration times bringing encouragement to people who are getting eaten up all week long! Then the lost will be drawn to Christ, for they will see that our news is indeed good news! God is able!

Romans 4:21 says that God is able to keep His promises. Let's hope like it!

Romans 11:23 says that God is able to convert those who are stubborn and opponents to Christianity. Our church can grow. Let's talk like it!

Romans 14:4 says that God is able to make us stand amid all the differences of opinion. We don't have to divide. Let's unite like it!

Second Corinthians 9:8 says that God is able to make us financially sufficient to provide for every good work. We don't have to be stingy. Let's give like it!

Jude 24 says that God is able to keep us from stumbling. We do not have to cave in to all the loose morals in this world. Let's resist like it!

Let's think like Paul. Look at Ephesians 3:20, 21. "Now to Him who is able to do all that we ask or think"—that's a big God, but that God is too small. That is not how Paul thought. "Now to Him who is able to do *beyond* all that we ask or think. . . ." Even that God is too small. "Now to Him who is able to do *abundantly beyond* all that we ask or think. . . ." Even that God is too small. Here is the good news: "Now to Him who is able to do *exceeding abundantly beyond all* that we ask or think, according to the power that works within us, to Him be the glory in the church and in Christ Jesus to all generations forever and ever. Amen."

CHAPTER 11

Who's Really Handicapped?
Mark 10:46-52; 12:41-44; 14:3-9

Nearly everywhere we go today, we see special ramps going into buildings. Nearby are special parking spaces marked with a picture of a wheelchair. Those remind us that we have handicapped people all around us.

There are many different ways to be handicapped. From our perspective, a person may be handicapped physically, materially, socially, or intellectually. But is it possible that we have misjudged who is really handicapped? And is it possible that our relationships to others have been somewhat hampered because we evaluate people too much according to the flesh?

Physically Handicapped?

As we watch Jesus' relationships with people, it dawns upon us that He did not view people to be handicapped the way others of His time viewed them. Let's look at three of those relationships.

And they came to Jericho. And as He was going out from Jericho with His disciples and a great multitude, a blind beggar named Bartimaeus, the son of Timaeus, was sitting by the road. And when he heard that it was Jesus the Nazarene, he began to cry out and say, "Jesus, Son of David, have mercy on me!" And many were sternly telling him to be quiet, but he kept crying out all the more, "Son of David, have mercy on me!" And Jesus stopped and said, "Call him here." And they called the blind man, saying to him, "Take courage, arise! He is calling for you." And casting aside his cloak, he jumped up, and came to Jesus. And answering him, Jesus said, "What do you want Me to do for you?" And the blind man said to Him, "Rabboni, I want to regain my sight!" And Jesus said to him, "Go your way; your faith has made you well." And immediately he regained his sight and began following Him on the road (Mark 10:46-52).

Do you ever feel as if you are in a crowd, having needs, but nobody notices, nobody cares, and nobody wants to slow down?

Crowds can be so impersonal; crowds can be so hurried; crowds can be so selfish; crowds can be so insensitive. Don't you sometimes feel that way even in the midst of a Christmas crowd that is going to and from a Christmas program, or in the midst of Christmas shopping?

But not everybody in a crowd has the crowd mentality. Jesus was in the midst of a great multitude on this day, but He took time for one individual person with a pressing need.

Jesus is always like that! There may be times that you may be just sitting by as was Bartimaeus. But there is not a time that Jesus passes by without noticing your need. Jesus never met an unimportant person, nor did He encounter an insignificant need—and that includes you and your needs!

Luke tells us that Bartimaeus was sitting by the roadside begging when he heard the crowd. Surely that must have lifted the hopes of that blind man. In any multitude of that day, some people would give to a beggar. And in a large multitude there may have been some who were able to give much. That blind man may have thought, "What a red-letter day this is going to be! This could be my best day ever!"

As the crowds went by, the blind man's curiosity arose; so he asked the people what this crowd meant (Luke 18:36). And the people answered, "Jesus of Nazareth is passing by" (Luke 18:37).

Jesus is still passing by. He is not just up in Heaven on some kind of eternal coffee break. He is still here. He still notices. He still cares. He's close by.

So that blind man's attention moved from the multitude to the Master. He had the ability to focus in on the right priority. The Master was around, and that blind man was not about to miss Him. Isn't it easy for us to let Jesus go past without reaching out to Him?

Suppose you had decided to take a backpacking trip into the wilderness and got lost. But in the middle of the night, you heard the search party coming your way. Let's suppose you were injured and about fifty feet off the trail. And the searchers started to pass by you. Wouldn't it be odd, foolish, useless, and unheard of to allow that search party to pass you by without your reaching out to them? But how often do we do that with the presence of God? We can learn a lot from Bartimaeus.

As Jesus was passing by, Bartimaeus took some initiative. He cried out, "Have mercy on me!" (Mark 10:47). At first, that just sounds natural to us who read it today. But let's not forget that Bartimaeus was really an outsider to that multitude. He was not a part of that crowd. He was not a member. As a matter of fact, he was a nobody, a person on the lowest rung of the social ladder. He was one of those persons that people would pass by and shake their heads at and thank God they were not like that person, and very easily neglect. By what right would this insignificant person think he could slow down this party that was on the way to the Passover? Why should he interrupt Jesus? Many people think like that today. Their low self-esteem makes them think that they have no claim on Jesus. But Jesus is always interruptible. Everyone has a right to Jesus. But He will not force himself upon us.

But that blind man had a better understanding of Jesus than did the people in the crowd. They called Jesus, "Jesus of Nazareth" (Luke 18:37). But the blind man called Jesus, "Son of David" (Luke 18:38; Mark 10:47). The term *Son of David* was a Messianic term. Is it possible that the blind man could see more clearly with his heart than those people could see with their eyes and heads? Although *Son of David* was a Messianic term, it was also a misunderstood term by the Jews. They linked up title with the kind of Messiah who would come as a military person as David did, and would expand the military kingdom as David had. So although that blind man understood Jesus as the Messiah, it's likely that he still had an inadequate understanding of the doctrine of God's Messiah. But it is interesting that God does not demand that we have our doctrine down pat before He stops and ministers to us in our needs. God never demands that we fully understand, but He does demand that we have faith. And Bartimaeus had faith! No one has to be a Bible scholar to cause Jesus to stop, notice, and help.

While the blind man wanted to open up to Jesus, the crowd wanted to close down that blind man's request. Mark says that "many were sternly telling him to be quiet" (Mark 10:48). Luke identifies them, "those who led the way." Those leaders may have been embarrassed that someone of Bartimaeus' status was asking for special privileges from Jesus. After all, the Bartimaeus kind of people often embarrass the leader kind of people. "We don't want to be bothered with people like you" was probably their inner thinking. So they told Bartimaeus to shut up.

Isn't it possible for leaders today to do the same thing? It is so easy for leaders to put a lid on the members of the church who are asking for God to do the impossible in their lives. It can be embarrassing for some leaders if members of the church believe that Jesus can actually bring sight to the blind, cleanness to the cancerous, and purity to the polluted.

That blind man was not going to allow the leaders to stand in his way to Jesus, so he began crying out all the more. While the leaders wanted him to become insignificant and fade away, he decided to become more intense. There is power in persistence. Bartimaeus was determined. Sometimes we will ask God once for something and then go our way and forget we have asked Him, and then we put the blame on Him for not meeting our needs. Several times, Jesus taught that God honors persistence. It is not because God does not hear us the first time, but it has something to do with measuring our own commitment to our own requests. Every parent knows how that works. We have had children who have asked us once for something that we did not provide at that particular moment. The child soon forgot about it and never asked again. He really did not need what he asked for, nor did he want it. He was in love with asking. But sometimes our children have asked over again and again. They have asked the right person for the right purpose and with the right persistence, and we as parents have come to understand that they are serious in being able to appreciate our giving what they asked. The more a person asks, the more He senses the need. And the more He senses the need, the more He may be filled with gratitude when that need is met.

That blind man kept asking, "and Jesus stopped" (Mark 10:49). What stopped Jesus? It was the cry of faith. Jesus pays attention to our faith. There was a great multitude in that crowd—perhaps three to four thousand people. But Jesus stopped for one person. One person stopped the crowd. Not only did that one person stop the crowd, but that one person also caused the crowd to change. Luke tells us that when they saw what Jesus did they "gave praise to God" (Luke 18:43).

What a change—from telling a man to shut up to praising God. Any single person today can stop his crowd and change it. I am glad that this one man did not cave in to the mentality of a few vocal ones or to the mentality of the crowd that was in a hurry. I am glad that he did not let those who led the way convince him that God did not have power that day to help him. His eyes were blind, but his heart could see. His mind could believe, and his mouth could ask.

Does your crowd need to be slowed down or stopped? Does it need to begin to praise God? Then perhaps it needs to see you reach out to God, asking for some big things from a big God. Jesus asked the blind man, "What do you want Me to do for you?" (Mark 10:51). What a question! But not everybody who makes requests to God is in touch with his real need. That blind man could have asked for a significant monetary gift from Jesus. But that would not have solved his problem. It would have helped him that day, but he would have had to return the next day to beg again. He could have asked for a white cane so he could get around better, or a seeing eye dog, or a braille Bible. But that blind man wanted to take some responsibility for living; so he asked for his sight. In a sense he was saying, "I am tired of not seeing. I want to see. I am tired of not working. I want to work. I am tired of receiving. I want to give to others." So he asked, believing that Jesus could do it. Somehow he believed that Jesus was big enough and powerful enough to meet a need no one else in his day could meet. He did not let the leaders of that multitude convince him that the devil had all the power on planet earth. Probably many of those leaders did not believe that Jesus could or would do it. Otherwise, they might not have told that man to keep still. How often we think too little, act too little, and pray too little. No wonder we get so little and seem to be proud of the little we receive.

Notice what happened to Jesus. He moved from passing by, to stopping, to listening, to saying, "You've got it!" And notice what happened to the blind man. He changed from sitting, begging, and crying to seeing, following, and glorifying God.

Who was really handicapped on that day? I would suggest to you that most of the people in the crowd were more handicapped than that blind man. A person who is physically handicapped is not necessarily personally handicapped. Just ask Joni Erickson. She is paralyzed from the neck down, but she has done more with her life than most people who can jog several miles before breakfast. Try to convince her that she is handicapped. Try to convince David Rothenberg who was set ablaze by his father when he was six years old. The book *David* is an outstanding book of courage, faith, determination, and wholeness. Some people today would turn their face away when they see David. His entire body shows all the evidences of having been critically burned. He still has no fingers, toes, or ears—but just try to convince him that he is handicapped. Many of the people who look at David, some of whom could be models with clear skin, are more handicapped personally than is David.

Materially Handicapped?

She was there, but she was lonely. She would go home to an empty place. No one was there to cuddle her; no one to put a log on the fire; no one to chat with. But she was there—amid the high and the mighty, and she walked along with them.

When her time came, she dropped in the two smallest coins, but they were all that she had. From all human analysis, she was materially handicapped.

Anyone who saw that surely would have thought, "What irresponsibility"; but Jesus was there. And He must have had a smile on His face. He must have thought, "What gratitude!" In fact, He said, "Truly I say to you, this poor widow put in more than all the contributors to the treasury" (Mark 12:43). *"More than all"* — what a compliment from Jesus! Who is really materially handicapped today? Is it those who cannot let go of what they possess, because they feel they are the sole owners? Or is it those who can let go, because they know God is the sole owner? It is one thing to be possessed by things, but another to be possessed by God. It is one thing to own wealth, but another thing for wealth to own us. Who is really handicapped—the one who has a lot, but is stingy, or the one who has little, but is generous? Who is really handicapped—the one who will not contribute to the work of God if it costs him pleasures, or the one who will give up pleasures for the work of God? Who is really handicapped—the one who has to be coaxed to give, or the one who gives voluntarily? Who is really handicapped—the one who will borrow money to buy automobiles that will not be around in a few years, or the one who would be willing to borrow for the work of the church, knowing that God's kingdom is eternal?

We have misused this portion of Scripture. We have called it the "widow's mite" to support the fact that we can just give a little to God's treasury. But the whole point of this is not that she gave so little, but that she gave so much. She gave "all she owned," all she had to live on. That is a lot of giving! So who is really handicapped materially—ones who feel that if they give a lot, they will have no means to live on, or the ones who feel that if they give all, God will provide?

Perhaps the work of God's kingdom is hindered more by those who really are materially handicapped today. They are the ones who hang on and will not let go. They promise to give to all kinds of financial companies (the ones that finance automobiles, braces for teeth, houses, credit cards, vacations, and you name it), but consider it an insult to be asked to make a commitment of a certain amount to the work of the church. The materially handicapped think nothing of paying a higher price for goods now than they used to because of inflation, but think it is materialistic of the church to expect people to increase their giving *every* single year. Often they feel that things in the world can be nice, but things in the church should be shabby, and they oppose those who feel that God's business deserves to have first-class equipment, facilities, and provisions as well as the devil's.

Who are really handicapped—those who are rich in goods and extravagant in self indulgence, or those who have few goods but are extravagant in sharing them?

Socially Handicapped?

It was an open-house reception for Jesus, as many receptions were in those days. So she slipped in unnoticed. She had to come unnoticed because she was really unwanted. She was from the wrong side of the tracks. The house was filled with the socially elite, but she did not mind. She knew why she had come. The woman was probably Mary, the sister of Martha and Lazarus (John 12:3). But she would have still been considered a socially handicapped person because she was a woman.

Greek philosophy had spread throughout that region. And Greek philosophers taught that women were inferior to men. Hesiod (8 B.C.) taught that women were the embodiment of evil. Semonides (7 B.C.) referred to women as swine. The Greek philosopher Herodotus (5 B.C.) taught that women were subordinate and should be exploited. Euripides (4 B.C.) taught that women and slaves were in the same category. Plato taught that men who were cowards and were unrighteous would be changed into women in the next life, and that mothers, because they are women, are a threat to the character of their children. Aristotle taught that men were by nature superior to women and that women were unfinished men. In fact, many Greek philosophers taught that the only way a woman could be a whole person was somehow to become a male.

Much of that negative thinking about women infiltrated into Jewish education and thought because of the way Alexander the Great, who was a student of Aristotle, spread the Greek culture through his campaigns. So by the time Jesus came, women were considered to be socially handicapped.

So this woman was from the wrong side of the social tracks. But that did not bother her. She knew why she had come. And so she took it out—that jar filled with perfume. The value was worth three hundred day's pay. That's a year's salary on today's market. That probably represented her life's savings—equal to an entire retirement account for today. Then she did the extravagant. She broke the jar and spilled all the contents on Jesus. She spent her total life's savings on this one event.

No doubt the men present thought, "What a waste!" In fact, they saw that the waste had no purpose to it at all (Mark 14:4). They began to put practicality thinking to this episode with the idea that the perfume could have been sold and given to the poor.

But Jesus was there. And He must have smiled and thought, "What gratitude!" He commended her, "She has done what she could" (Mark 14:8). But what she did seems so extravagant!

Doesn't love have a certain amount of extravagance to it? Doesn't love reach out and do things at the moment when it may be the only chance to do it? Doesn't love take risks?

Is it true that Christianity is to have no extravagance to it whatsoever? Why can we put plush carpeting in our homes, but fuss if we spend a few extra bucks for carpeting in the church building? Why do we say that if something is spiritual, it should not look attractive or have any extravagance attached to it? Why have we taught that class is carnality and quality is quackery in the church? Why do we put God's name on display in what looks like leftovers, afterthoughts, hand-me-downs, and second-hand stuff? It is one thing to be good stewards; it is another thing to be stingy. Why should preachers receive less salary than garbage collectors? Why should members go on strike for a better retirement plan while refusing to give their church staff any at all? Why should members ask about the hospitalization plan where they work but think it is not spiritual for the preacher to ask about one for himself and his family?

This woman showed that love can be extravagant even though not totally understood. In this act, she was far less handicapped than the socially elite who wanted to keep their fingers so tight on the purses that nothing out of the ordinary would ever get spent in a way that honors the splendor and the awesomeness of the living God. Have we honored mediocrity and shabbiness in our committee votes?

Jesus said it to the blind man when He said, "Your faith has made you well" (Mark 10:52). He said it about the widow when He told His disciples that she had given "more than all" (Mark 12:43). He said it again when He said the extravagant woman had "done a good deed to Me.... She has done what she could.... that also which this woman has done shall be spoken of in memory of her" (Mark 14:6, 8, 9). What Jesus said in all three of these situations was that what appears to be a physical handicap, a material handicap, and a social handicap does not really need to be a handicap at all. It is not what is on the outside and can be measured that matters, but rather what is on the inside.

The most liberated people are those who are freed from their situations to reach out toward Jesus, to give unselfishly, and even to waste extravagantly because they have a relationship with God that cannot be fettered.

How handicapped are we?—with our 20/20 vision, savings accounts, and acceptable social standing?

CHAPTER 12

From the Last Supper to the Marriage Banquet
Mark 14:12—16:20

The Last Supper

Jesus' last night with His disciples must have been a tough one for Him. He had invested His life in those men, and they had invested their lives with Him. They had shared happy times and grieving times; they had shared ordinary times and miraculous meals; they had traveled together, eaten together, gone to weddings together, and no doubt spent many times sleeping under the stars together. In short, they had spent time on the front lines together.

Anyone who has been in military service knows the kinds of closeness that people have with one another as they share those various kinds of experiences. It has been nearly forty years since I left Korea, but I remember the lump in my throat when I departed from those guys with whom we had all shared so much. And after all of those years, I still remember their names, although I have not seen them since. That's amazing, for I have forgotten the names of some people I have met within the past year.

Jesus knew this would be His last night with those men. So He shared with them a real love-feast. It was the Passover, which recalls the time that God saved His people from the Egypt of their day. They had been enslaved and mistreated.

Now Jesus would become the new Passover, who would save God's people from a different kind of slavery and a different kind of exploitation. God would save His people from the slavery to sin and the exploitation from the devil.

How would God do it? He would do it by allowing His Son to take the rap for us. And when that happened, He would drive a wall between us and Satan and break down the wall that had separated mankind from God.

Some of Jesus' most memorable words were spoken at this time. It was at this time that He said such words as:

"Let not your heart be troubled; believe in God, believe also in Me. In My Father's house are many dwelling places; if it were not so, I would have told you; for I go to prepare a place for you" (John 14:1, 2).

"I am the way, and the truth, and the life; no one comes to the Father, but through Me" (John 14:6).

"Truly, truly, I say to you, he who believes in Me, the works that I do shall he do also; and greater works than these shall he do; because I go to the Father" (John 14:12).

"If you love Me, you will keep My commandments" (John 14:15).

"A new commandment I give to you, that you love one another, even as I have loved you, that you also love one another" (John 13:34).

"I will not leave you as orphans; I will come to you" (John 14:18).

"Peace I leave with you; My peace I give to you; not as the world gives, do I give to you. Let not your heart be troubled, nor let it be fearful" (John 14:27).

"I am the true vine.... Abide in Me, and I in you. As the branch cannot bear fruit of itself, unless it abides in the vine, so neither can you, unless you abide in Me" (John 15:1, 4).

"These things I have spoken to you, that My joy may be in you, and that your joy may be made full" (John 15:11).

"Greater love has no one that this, that one lay down his life for his friends" (John 15:13).

"But when He, the Spirit of truth, comes, He will guide you into all the truth; for He will not speak on His own initiative, but whatever He hears, He will speak; and He will disclose to you what is to come. He shall glorify Me; for He shall take of Mine, and shall disclose it to you" (John 16:13, 14).

"In the world you have tribulation, but take courage; I have overcome the world" (John 16:33).

"Sanctify them in the truth; Thy word is truth" (John 17:17).

"As Thou didst send Me into the world, I also have sent them into the world" (John 17:18).

"I do not ask in behalf of these alone, but for those also who believe in Me through their word; that they may all be one; even as Thou, Father, art in Me, and I in Thee, that they also may be in Us; that the world may believe that Thou didst send Me" (John 17:20, 21).

What a night of remembrances that night turned out to be! It was on that night that Jesus washed the disciples' feet. What an act of humility and what an act of service!

But also on that night, Jesus instituted the memorial feast that we call the Lord's Supper, the Communion, the Eucharist, and the Last Supper. Some congregations observe this every Lord's Day in remembrance of Jesus. Other congregations observe it monthly, quarterly, and/or on special occasions. Jesus said, "Do this, as often as you drink it, in remembrance of Me" (1 Corinthians 11:25). Paul observed that as often as we do this, we proclaim the Lord's death until He comes (1 Corinthians 11:26).

People are so forgetful and people are also so inclined to take too much credit for themselves. Without a regular observance of the Lord's Supper, we can more easily forget that Jesus died on our behalf. We can forget why it is that people who are so diverse are now united in one body. We can also begin to think that we are in God's family because of our works, our education, our accomplishments, or our service. But the Lord's Supper reminds us that we are saved by grace through faith. It reminds us of undeserved forgiveness.

The Lord's Supper also reminds us that we are people of the New Covenant and not the Old Covenant. What celebrations that ought to bring! For the Old Covenant required trips to Jerusalem, a bull given every year for sins, and a host of other legalities that would burden us. The Lord's Supper is indeed a time for celebration.

The Lord's Supper is also a time to remember that Jesus did not just die, but that He arose. We do not worship a dead saint, but a living Savior. He not only arose from the dead, but He is coming back for us.

The Lord's Supper is also a time to remember that the people around us in Christ are united to us. Our unity is because of Christ, not because of conformity to one another's ideas, pet peeves, hobby horses, or doctrines. Partaking of the one bread is to remind us that we are one body (1 Corinthians 10:17).

To partake of the Lord's Supper also reminds us of our responsibilities toward one another. The people of Corinth began to pervert their celebration of the Lord's Supper by not expressing real unity to one another. As a matter of fact, they had fusses and fights going on at the same time they were partaking of what they called "the Lord's Supper." But the Lord's Supper is a meal of unity, not disunity. It is a meal of love, not animosities. It is a meal for the family, not for factions (1 Corinthians 11:17-34). It was after Paul had discussed the significance of the Lord's Supper that he moved immediately to discuss the relevance of every member in the body of Christ (1 Corinthians 12). No one should feel either superior or inferior to the others. We are gifted differently for the common good of all (1 Corinthians 12:7). So sharing in the Lord's Supper involves not only thinking about Jesus on the cross two thousand years ago—although that is a must—but also thinking about God's people around us who make up His ongoing body in our world today. The Lord's Supper is a time to reaffirm our commitment to both the Messiah and to the members of the Messiah's body.

The Garden

From that supper, Jesus went to the Garden of Gethsemane, where He wrestled with the decision of whether or not to go through with dying in our place. His inner feelings said, "No!" Can't we understand that? The cross was painful. The cross was disgraceful. The cross was lonely. The cross signaled alienation. The cross signaled a curse. Would we want to go through any of that for others?

So Jesus did not let His feelings have the last word on that night. Instead, He allowed His commitment to have priority, "Not what I will, but what Thou wilt" (Mark 14:36).

Feelings are certainly a part of Christianity. But we must live our Christian confession out of commitment, not just out of feeling. There are times when we may not feel like getting up, going to worship, giving a significant gift, serving someone in need, praying, or being faithful to some other commitment. But commitment must win over feelings.

None of us should forget that on that night, God said no to Jesus in order to say yes to us. God would watch His Son die so He could see us live forever.

In a sense, each of us has a garden type of experience every day. For every day, we have to make the decision whether or not to deny self, take up our cross, and follow Jesus. Every day, we have to decide whether or not our decisions will be made primarily for self-preservation, self-good, self-benefit, self-comfort, self-convenience, self-desire—or for the benefit of others in need. Husbands and wives have to make that decision for each other. Parents have to make that decision for children. Students have to make that decision in the classroom. Children have to make that decision with parents. Employees have to make that decision with employers. Employers have to make that decision with employees. The real issue in the Garden experience is this: for whom are we living—self or others, under the umbrella of God's will?

The Cross

It was not the pain of the nails that caused Jesus to be reluctant in that garden. It was not the shame that He would have in front of others. It was not the physical death. Jesus knew that the pain would be temporary. Jesus had lived much of His ministry being rejected by others and thus being ridiculed and shamed and falsely charged. Jesus knew that the physical death would be temporary, for He had prophesied that after three days He would rise again.

Then what was it about the cross that caused Jesus to pray, "If it's possible, let this cup pass from me"? It was the separation from His Heavenly Father.

Jesus would not just die a physical death on that cross. He would die "real death." Real death is to be separated from God because of sin. And Jesus would take our sins in His body and taste separation in our place. That's what Paul meant when he wrote, "He made Him who knew no sin to be sin on our behalf, that we might become the righteousness of God in Him" (2 Corinthians 5:21). That's what Peter meant when he wrote, "He

137

himself bore our sins in His body on the cross, that we might die to sin and live to righteousness; for by His wounds you were healed" (1 Peter 2:24). That's what the writer of Hebrews meant when he wrote, "By the grace of God He might taste death for everyone" (Hebrews 2:9). That's what the prophet prophesied when he wrote, "The Lord has caused the iniquity of us all to fall on Him" (Isaiah 53:6).

The death that sin earns (Romans 6:23) is separation from God the Father. And God wants that separation to be erased. So He sent His Son to die in our place so that in Christ we are reunited to God (Ephesians 2:11-22). But in order to take our place in death, Jesus himself had to experience it. That means He had to become separated from His Father. That's why He cried on the cross when He was breathing His last, "My God, My God, why hast Thou forsaken Me?" (Mark 15:34). Jesus tasted Hell for us, for Hell is total separation from the Father.

How would God answer that question, "Why hast Thou forsaken Me?" God answered it with a four-letter word—love! "For God so loved the world, that He gave His only begotten Son" (John 3:16).

The death of Jesus on the cross for you affirms your worth in the eyes of God. God created you, and God does not create junk. Jesus died for you, and Jesus did not die for junk. God bought you in Christ's death, and God does not buy junk—as we are so expert at doing. Jesus arose from the dead and went to the Father so that He could send the Spirit to us. And the Holy Spirit does not live inside of junk. Jesus is coming back for us, and Jesus does not come back for junk.

While the death of Christ on the cross looked like the end, it was really a new beginning. It began the Christian era. It began the possibility of new life for you and me. It began a new relationship with mankind to God. Of course, it was also an end—not the end of Jesus, but the end of the old era, the Old Covenant, the old way to relate to God, our old commitment to Satan, and the old way to live.

The Resurrection of Jesus—and Ours

Christ died with no sins of His own in His body. But He died with our sins in His body. Since the wages of sin is death, those sins in His body caused separation between Him and the Father.

But when God forgave us our sins in Christ's self-sacrifice, then

Jesus had no sins left in His body. So the Holy Spirit re-entered Jesus' body and brought Jesus up from the grave. And that same Spirit can live in us. And if that Spirit lives in us, that Spirit will also bring us up from the grave into eternal life.

> However, you are not in the flesh but in the Spirit, if indeed the Spirit of God dwells in you. But if anyone does not have the Spirit of Christ, he does not belong to Him. And if Christ is in you, though the body is dead because of sin, yet the spirit is alive because of righteousness. But if the Spirit of Him who raised Jesus from the dead dwells in you, He who raised Christ Jesus from the dead will also give life to your mortal bodies through His Spirit who indwells you" (Romans 8:9-11).

Jesus' resurrection is a validation of the truth of Christianity. If Jesus had not risen from the dead, then the apostle's movement would have stopped on that day of the crucifixion. After all, those apostles were scared and scattered. There would have been no motivation to continue for the cause of Jesus apart from the resurrection. It would have been too dangerous, senseless, and irrelevant, for the death of Jesus would have affirmed that He was not the Messiah. And those men were not interested in just starting another religion. They were interested in being a part of the ministry of the true Messiah. They were not about to give up Judaism for a cult. But they would be a part of the fulfilment of Judaism in the promised Messiah.

Anyone who wants to deny the actual resurrection of Jesus two thousand years ago has to deny too much. He would have to deny the following: (1) the fact that no one in the first century denied the historical resurrection of Jesus; (2) the crowds that saw Jesus, talked with Him, ate with Him, and touched Him after He arose; (3) the beginning of the Church, rather than the ending of a movement; (4) the change in the lives of the apostles from being terrified to being courageous; (5) the fact that the soldiers were paid a large sum of money in order to make up a lie concerning the disappearance of Jesus' body; (6) the fact that fifty days later in Jerusalem, which was crowded with many people who had been there for the crucifixion and many of whom evidently saw the resurrection, did not, less than two months later, deny the resurrection when Peter preached that tremendous sermon affirming it; (7) the fact that years later when Paul spoke to Felix and Festus about the resurrection, they did not deny its reality.

Historical reality affirms that Jesus of Nazareth arose from the grave. And the testimony of witnesses affirms that He ascended into Heaven. He prophesied He would—and He did!

That ascension is imperial evidence that He never died again! He is eternal! He is "the Alpha and the Omega . . . who is and who was and who is to come, the Almighty" (Revelation 1:8).

And He will come with the clouds, and every eye shall see Him, and every knee shall bow to His Lordship. It is foolish to refuse to bow now, when we will all bow then!

And when Jesus comes again, He will take His people to an eternal gathering and into an eternal life. He shall wipe away every tear from our eyes, there shall no longer be any death; there shall no longer be any mourning, or crying, or pain; the first things have passed away. He will make all things new!

We will walk on streets of gold. We will live in mansions. We will always be in the presence of God. We will be in the midst of a perfect environment, a perfect crowd, a perfect life-style, and a perfect relationship. There will be no pollution, sin, disappointments, depression, exploitation, cheating, or loss of any kind. We will become heirs of God and joint heirs with Christ. The universe and the universes will be ours to enjoy.

In Christ, there is victory. In Christ, we are winning right now! So why not celebrate? Why not allow our emotions to burst out with praise and glory and singing and shouts? During athletic games, we celebrate when our team is winning. As a matter of fact, the whole auditorium can become a place of pandemonium. I have noticed that it becomes silent whenever our side is losing. Folks, we are not losing. We are winning. Even the Psalmist in the Old Testament knew that God's people were winning even though they had temporary setbacks. No wonder He spoke about clapping of hands, the shouting of voices, the leaping with joy, the singing of new songs. Those who want to put a clamp on any kind of emotional expression of God's people should take a backseat with their opinionated deadness. For God is great! He is powerful! He is almighty! He is winning! And He deserves to be worshipped with celebration of hilarious praise.

At that time, we will participate in a fantastic wedding feast (Revelation 19:9). It will be a feast of joy. It will be a feast of celebration. It will be a feast of victory. It will be a feast of thanksgiving. It will be a feast of renewing our commitment to our Husband—Jesus Christ!

He will come for His "bride adorned for her husband" (Revelation 21:2). We will see His beauty. We will see His glory. We will see His splendor. And we will share His splendor, for we will be changed into His likeness (1 John 3:2).

What an experience—from the Last Supper to an eternal feast with Him. From death to resurrection; from the cross to the crown; from mortality to immortality; from the earthly to the Heavenly.

It is all ours in Christ, for there is "no condemnation for those who are in Christ Jesus" (Romans 8:1). In Christ, we are conquerors—yea, more than conquerors.

No wonder Paul could be confident in the midst of difficulties, joyful in the midst of pain, encouraged in the midst of persecution. He knew what was ahead of Him, and He had made a commitment to press on to the prize of the high calling of God. And He did it with this conviction, which must be our conviction. Let us encourage one another with it. Let us remind one another of it. And let us live in it.

> For I am convinced that neither death, nor life, nor angels, nor principalities, nor things present, nor things to come, nor powers, nor height, nor depth, nor any other created thing, shall be able to separate us from the love of God, which is in Christ Jesus our Lord (Romans 8:38, 39).

If God allowed Christ to die in our place on the cross—and He did—then know ye this, **"God causes all things to work together for good to those who love God, to those who are called according to His purpose"** (Romans 8:28).

CHAPTER 13

Who Is on Our Side?
(A Summary Look at Jesus)

Christianity had not been advancing very long when "the kings of the earth took their stand, and the rulers were gathered together against the Lord, and against His Christ" (Acts 4:26). That opposition against God was hurled directly against God's people.

The Christians at Rome, to whom Mark first wrote, must have felt that all the power structures in their world were gathered together against God, for they certainly seemed to be against Christians.

It was to those people that the apostle Paul wrote, "If God is for us, who can be against us?" (Romans 8:31, NIV).

"Who can be against us?" What kind of question is that? Those Christians in Rome knew full well who could be against them. Nero was against them. Popularity of the people had turned against them. The wild beasts were turned loose against them.

However, even though those experiences brought pain, inconveniences, and physical death, compared to God, those opposers were like a legless and blind retarded ant up against an elephant.

That's why Paul wrote to those people in Rome, "But in all these things we overwhelmingly conquer through Him who loved us" (Romans 8:37).

The one who was on the side of those Roman Christians in the midst of their storm is the same one who is with us in the midst of our experiences.

But just who is this one on our side? In this chapter, we want to pull together many of the snapshots that Mark gave us of Jesus. When all of those snapshots are put together, we should give Jesus a standing ovation and with one accord echo the words of John:

> For whatever is born of God overcomes the world; and this is the victory that has overcome the world—our faith. And who is the one who overcomes the world, but he who believes that Jesus is the Son of God?

You are from God, little children, and have overcome them; because greater is He who is in you than he who is in the world (1 John 5:4, 5; 4:4).

He Is Greater Than Autonomy

The more powerful we get, the easier it is for us to feel that we really do not need others. We have nearly idolized independence in this country. That Jesus would not cave in to that mentality is seen by many events in His life.

1. His Baptism (Mark 1:9). In His baptism, Jesus identified with both God and with His fellowman. He had no trouble with being baptized by one lesser than He (John the Baptist). Jesus also submitted himself to God. That is one of the significant meanings of baptism for any person today. Baptism is also a commitment to live our lives in service to other people as a representative of the Lord. In baptism we are delivered from the damnation of our own egos and are linked up with God and with all of God's people.

2. His Disciples. Jesus' refusal to be autonomous is also seen in the calling of disciples to be with Him, to follow Him, and to participate in a ministry that is always to be larger than that of one person. Too many leaders in local congregations try to go it alone. It is easy to look around and see others who may not be as competent as we and then just neglect them. When Jesus looked around, He saw everyone less competent than He. But He tapped their potential. He lit their fuses. He fellowshiped with them, ate with them, and traveled with them. He was not about to be a Lone-ranger Son of God.

3. His Commission (Mark 6:7ff). Not only did Jesus call people to be His disciples, He also sent them out in His ministry. It is one thing to call people to our classes to study under us, it is another thing to let them go into significant ministries without being threatened by their success. Jesus still calls disciples to be with Him and to go for Him (Mark 16:15). He is not threatened by us. In fact, He empowers us.

4. His Prayer Life. Here is further proof of Jesus' lack of independence. Not only did He continue to maintain a relationship with people around Him, but He also maintained a relationship with God. Jesus never thought that just because things were working in His ministry, He did not have to maintain continual contact with His Heavenly Father. His prayer time with the Father impressed His disciples as much as any aspect of His life. The disciples never once asked Jesus to teach them to preach, although they heard Him preach in a way that held multitudes in the palms of His hands. They never once asked Jesus to teach them to teach, although they heard Him teach in a way that both the religious leaders and the little children were spellbound. They never once asked Jesus to teach them to do miracles, although they saw Him work unbelievable wonders. They never once asked Jesus to teach them how to field questions, although they heard Him deal flawlessly with questions and criticisms. But after they had been with Him for a while, they did ask, "Teach us to pray" (Luke 11:1).

Are we known as a praying people? Do we spend as much time in prayer as in reading the Word? Do we make our prayers specific? Are prayer meetings as well attended in the church as musical concerts?

The one who is on our side is one who refused to become autonomous. He showed His identity with God and others in baptism, He showed His interdependence upon fellowman in calling them as disciples and sending them, and He continued to show His dependence upon God in His prayer life. And He expects us to follow Him.

He Is Greater Than Temptations

Immediately following Jesus' baptism, He went into the wilderness and was tempted by the devil (Mark 1:12, 13). In fact, we are told elsewhere that He was tempted in every point that we are tempted (Hebrews 4:15). As He was greater than the temptations of His day, He who lives within us is still greater than any of the temptations in our day.

How are we tempted today? James tells us that we are tempted when we are lured and enticed by our own desires (James 1:14). I have never been tempted with anything that I did not desire. Our basic desires were given to us by God and are good. Those desires include such things as hunger, thirst, sex, and security. God, who gave us those good desires, also gave us a wonderful world in which those desires could be fulfilled. To fulfill the desire for hunger, He gave us a world with food. To fulfill the desire of thirst, He gave us a world with water. To fulfill the desire for sex, he gave us male and female. To fulfill the desire for security, He gave us love, himself, and others.

But God also put some guardrails around His world. As long as we stay within those guardrails, we can have those desires met by

God's world in meaningful ways that benefit us rather than destroy us. When we go beyond the guardrails, we head for a crash. The guardrail for hunger is not being a glutton. The guardrail for thirst is no drunkenness. The guardrail for sex is marriage. But Satan comes along and begins to tempt us just a bit beyond those guardrails. When he lures us, he baits the hook as fishermen do. It looks so good and authentic, but what we do not see is the hook on the inside. When he entices us, he makes it sound so good as hunters do with their manufactured duck calls. Those ducks hear what sounds authentic and see decoys on the lake that look authentic. But what they have not seen or heard are the hunters behind the duck blinds ready to destroy them.

Jesus did not permit Satan to get Him beyond guardrails. And God has given us His Word, His Spirit, and His church to keep us within His guardrails today. The one who is in us is indeed greater than the one who is in the world.

He Is Greater Than Demons

He cast demons out (Mark 1:23-26, 34; 5:1-13; 9:25-27). Demons are the helpers of the devil. They are as real as are angels from God. They can influence from the outside through various means or possess a person from the inside. The more Christianity advances in a culture, the less evident the activities of the demons seem to be. But they are still evident, as seen in the kind of mass immoral atrocities that go on. When a person receives Jesus as Savior and receives the gift of the Holy Spirit, all unholy spirits leave. It is an impossibility for the demons to reside in the same body with the Holy Spirit. However, Satan does not give up on us. He seeks to influence us while not possessing us. But the one who is in us (the Holy Spirit) is greater than the one who is in the world.

He Is Greater Than Disease

He healed all kinds of diseases, from fever to leprosy and paralysis. He is God's great physician.

Although the fatality rate for all of us is one hundred percent (we will all eventually die physically), the presence of Jesus can still affect our physical health as well as our spiritual health. *Disease* literally means dis-ease. Disease is caused by a diseasement or disharmony or imbalance. Jesus can help bring harmony and balance to our lives.

Many of the teachings of the Bible can affect our physical well-being. For instance, Proverbs is filled with verses that talk about how our tongues can actually affect our stomachs and our health. Proverbs says that "a joyful heart is good medicine" (Proverbs 17:22). Paul wrote that physical exercise has some effect, but godliness is profitable for all things (1 Timothy 4:8). We are told that by Jesus' scourging we are healed (Isaiah 53:5), and "by His wounds you were healed" (1 Peter 2:24). Notice it says, "you *were* healed." In Jesus, healing is a reality.

We misunderstand ourselves if we think that our total self is just wrapped up in a physical body. The real self is the inner man inside of that body. Jesus brings healing to that inner man so that while the outer body may be decaying, the inner man can be renewed day by day (2 Corinthians 4:16).

Every Christian ought to say to himself many times, "I am healed. I am healed. I am healthy." And he should say that even though his physical body is going through devastating disharmony. A person is more than his physical body. Jesus' superiority over disease is far more than just reducing fever, getting rid of colds, or clearing up cancer.

John Quincy Adams expressed it when he was once asked how he was. He replied, "The house John Quincy Adams is in is decaying and falling apart, but John Quincy Adams is quite all right—indeed, quite all right."

He Is Greater Than Sin

He came as God in flesh forgiving sins (John 1:1, 14). God specializes in letting go of the past. God promises that He is able to forgive us of our sins and to forget them. And when God forgets about something, it is gone from His recall forever. Many Christians have never really accepted the refreshing cleansing of God's forgiveness. They have gone through the motions, said the words, been baptized, and attended worship services for years, but never internalized their forgiveness by God. So they keep hanging on to the guilt that God had already placed on Jesus on the cross. Many people need to accept God's forgiveness even though they think they are unworthy of it.

Not only does Jesus forgive sins, but He also tells us to forgive (Mark 11:25). Forgiving another heals us as much as it heals the person who has sinned against us.

He Is Greater Than Turmoil

When the gale was blowing outside, Jesus was asleep on a pillow in the boat (Mark 4:37-41). The one who is in that boat in peace is the one who is in us with His peace. A secret for allowing that peace to be potent in the midst of the gale around us is found in Philippians 4:4-9. We are to have the power of positive thinking and possibility thinking operating, so that even though tough stuff is going on, we can look for the positive and rejoice (verse 4). We can commit to ourselves that with Him, we are going to stay in control (verse 5). We can replace anxiety with asking God in prayer (verse 6). Then the peace of God becomes the sentry on duty at the doorway of our hearts and minds. And with that kind of peace, we can think about the positive and not the negative, concerning what is right and not what is wrong around us, about what is lovely and not what is ugly, about what is of good reputation instead of all the garbage that we could gossip about, about what is excellent instead of what is incompetent and unworthy (verse 8). With that kind of inner commitment, "the God of peace shall be with you" (verse 9).

He Is Greater Than Traditions

He did not allow the traditional way of thinking and the traditional way of living to dictate His kind of character or ministry. He did not allow others' ideas about the Sabbath day to prevent Him from doing good on the Sabbath. He did not make it a priority to live for rituals while neglecting people's needs. He did not feel He nor His apostles had to fast just because it was the traditional thing to do, regardless of the needs of the moment (Mark 2:18-22).

Jesus expects us to be bigger than traditions, for He who lives in us is greater than the one who lives in the world—even though that one may be one of the various traditions that we are expected to keep.

Jesus expects us not to trap God inside the small boxes of our traditions when those traditions keep the love, compassion, purity, power, and presence of God isolated from others. The one who is in us is greater than the traditions around us.

He Is Greater Than Conflicts

Jesus' conflicts came from surprising sources. He had conflicts with some of the most respected religious leaders of His day

(Mark 12:13, 18). He had conflict with His own family members (Mark 3:21, 31-35). Most of his conflicts from religious leaders came because He did not mouth or practice the traditions that they had been accustomed to doing. His family members began to think He was insane and wanted to take Him home.

Having conflicts is certainly not new within the church. And they can come to us from the most surprising people. But conflict resolution has not always been done with Christlikeness.

Every congregation ought to study the situations that brought Jesus into conflict and then study His reactions. Jesus dealt with issues and principles and never with personalities. He never sought to defend himself, but only the issues and principles at stake. His answers were short, gentle, and to the point. They brought the will and character of God the Father into the people's sight. For instance, when He was criticized for eating with sinners and publicans, He simply answered, "It is not those who are healthy who need a physician, but those who are sick" (Mark 2:17). When He was criticized for doing good on the Sabbath, He said shortly, but sweetly, "The Sabbath was made for man, and not man for the Sabbath" (Mark 2:27). That is not a bad answer to many tradition keepers.

He Is Greater Than Rejection

Jesus was bigger than rejection. The kindest and finest man was not always wanted. Even His hometown wanted to get rid of Him after He preached there (Luke 4:16-29). The people of ten cities (the Decapolis) wanted Him to get out of that whole area after He had cast those demons into swine (Mark 5:1-20).

What was Jesus' reaction to that? Too many times, we let our egos get in the way. We fight against rejection. We dig in our heels and are determined to stay at all costs. What we really mean by most of that is that we are going to have it our own way. When His hometown wanted to get rid of Him, Jesus just left. When the people of Decapolis wanted Him out of their area, He just got into a boat and left. That's maturity! And especially is it maturity when some of that happened after Jesus had become so popular among the people. It is super tough to be popular with the masses and then not be wanted where you are ministering. To have to leave an area is a loss of face. Others might find out the circumstances. But Jesus trusted in the bigness of God. He never got onto bandwagons. He never defended himself. He never blamed others. Isn't it interesting that when He returned to Decapolis, the people (probably the same people who had asked Him to leave before) flocked to Him (Mark 5:17, 8:1)?

I wonder if that would have happened had Jesus left with a chip on His shoulder and a sharp sword in His mouth. Jesus is greater than charges hurled at Him personally. It is one thing to be in conflict over issues, but it is quite another thing when people are attacking you personally—particularly when you have become rather popular.

However, it is a general rule of thumb that the more a person does in public, the more vulnerable he is to being attacked personally. The more he does what is really influential and effective, the more some people want to cut him down. And the only way some people know how to put up barriers is by loading the mouth with damaging bullets and firing away.

At one time His own family members had attacked Him personally by claiming that He had lost His senses (Mark 3:21). Religious leaders claimed He was empowered by demons (Mark 3:22). Other religious leaders claimed that He had no authority for the kind of things He was doing (Mark 11:27-33). Other people simply laughed at Him (Mark 5:40). Perhaps the finest way to measure the bigness of a man is to watch his reaction towards the littleness of others. We can never really control another person's actions towards us. We can wish those actions were not taking place. We can pray those actions would cease. We can try to live in a way that those actions don't come. But we cannot control them. However, we can control our reactions. If we don't, we have really lost control to other people.

If we permit the action of others to determine our reactions, then we have let them be in control of us. They may not even realize they are in control of us. And we may not realize it. When we are attacked personally, our first thought should be, "Who is going to be in control of this reaction—those people or the Holy Spirit? And the one who is in me is greater than the one who is in the world—and greater than those personal attacks. I will allow them to see the fruit of God's Spirit, not the foolishness of my spirit."

He Is Greater Than Personal Grief

Jesus had times of grief. He no doubt grieved when He heard John the Baptist had been executed. That is probably part of the reason He told His apostles to get away for a while (Mark 6:14, 31). It is quite clear that he was filled with grief in the Garden of Gethsemane (Mark 14:34). But in both of those occasions, He did not allow grief to lead Him around as though grief were the master and He were a puppy dog on its leash. In both cases, He responded to grief the same way—He prayed and then served the needs of the people.

It is important for us to recognize grief and not pretend it doesn't exist. But it is also significant for us to crawl outside of that grief and invest our lives in meeting some of the felt needs of others. That turns the eyes off self to others. It replaces grief with a bit of joy. It replaces misery with a bit of meaningfulness. It replaces the paralysis that grief can bring with practices that love can do.

He Is Greater Than Positioning Tactics of Others

Those on the inner circle—His apostles—knew how to argue about which one of them was the greatest. They knew how to jockey for status positions (Mark 9:33-37; 10:35-45).

It is interesting that the first time we know about the apostles arguing about who is the greatest was right after Jesus told them He was going to be killed (Mark 9:30-37). Instead of being filled with grief upon hearing that, they immediately began to argue about which one of them was the greatest. In fact, they did the same thing at the last supper, when Jesus again prophesied He was going to die and let them know it was going to be soon (Luke 22:21-32). Jesus could have really taken that as a personal threat. But Jesus wasn't paranoid. He did not say, "Who's the greatest? I'm the greatest and never forget it." He never thought, "Those guys are trying to up-seat Me and take over." Without any kind of personal threat, Jesus answered those positioning tactics in a way that got to the issue without defending himself. On one occasion, He put a child in their midst and claimed that one who is willing to become like a child is the greatest (Mark 9:36, 37). A child is teachable. A child is submissive. A child forgets wrongs done against him quickly. A child trusts. On another occasion, Jesus let them know that the one who was willing to serve all the others would be considered the greatest (Mark 10:42-45). Staff members at a church can learn a lot by how Jesus handled potential positioning tactics. The one who lives in us is greater than all the positioning tactics around us.

He Is Greater Than Trick Questions

Many times people questioned Jesus just to trip Him up—just to embarrass Him—just to create opposition against His answers (Mark 12:13-34). That tactic has never stopped. Church leaders are often asked leading questions for the primary purpose of putting those leaders on the spot and engineering some people in the crowd, if not the whole audience, against those leaders.

But Jesus never took those questions personally, although He knew the motives behind the people who asked them. Instead, He answered them clearly for the purpose of giving people correct insight. He did not think ahead of time how He thought His audience wanted Him to answer the question. Although realizing that His answers might not be accepted by any or all, Jesus nevertheless answered those questions for the purpose of providing God's insight. While they saw it as a way to trap Him, He saw it as a way to help them in understanding. Their evil motives gave Him an opportunity to do good things through that kind of teaching.

He Is Greater Than a Sectarian Spirit

The potential of denominationalism, which builds walls to keep others out, was present very early, even while Jesus was still physically on earth traveling with His disciples (Mark 9:38-50). God's people do meet in different places and do have different opinions. But denominationalism, which fails to see a brother in a different location or meeting place just because he is not in one's own group, is sin. God sent Jesus to unite His people under one head, not divide them by sectarian attitudes. Anyone who is in Christ is automatically connected to everyone else who is in Christ. There is only one body, although many different expressions of that body.

The attitude of separation into different denominations that refuse to recognize others as fellow brothers and sisters can begin within our smaller groups themselves. Many times, we get upset with one another, argue against one another, and start blaming one another. Eventually, then, we divide from one another. That is why Jesus concluded this section against potential sectarianism by saying to the men within that small group of apostles, "Have salt within yourselves, and be at peace with one another" (Mark 9:50).

Only Mark records this teaching from Jesus. The Christians in Rome surely needed to hear this, for in the midst of their difficulties, it would have been easy for them to go after each other because of different ways some had reacted to the Roman persecution and charges.

What does it mean to "have salt in yourselves"? Salt is a preservative. We put salt on good meat to keep it from rotting. Christians are to be salt to one another. Touching one another, encouraging one another, teaching one another, fellowshiping with one another, and loving one another for the purpose of helping to preserve one another. Salt is also a healing substance. Christians are to pour the healing attitudes into one another rather than to keep the wounds open and alive and allow them to fester. Salt was used in the Old Testament when offering sacrifices. Christians are to be willing to sacrifice for one another as living sacrifices.

Christians who have denominated themselves from one another with an exclusive attitude have been able to do that because, through the years, we have ignored Jesus' teachings. "Salt is good; but if the salt becomes unsalty, with what will you make it salty again? Have salt in yourselves, and be at peace with one another" (Mark 9:50).

It is interesting that Jesus prefaces this teaching by telling His disciples that whatever it is in their lives that causes them to stumble should be cut out of their lives (Mark 9:42-45). And in this context, the stumbling has to do with a sectarian attitude that will not include those whom God has included.

He Is Greater Than Exclusiveness

The religious leaders of Jesus' day were experts at excluding people. Jesus was an expert at including people. His Spirit of inclusiveness was demonstrated to women, sinners, Syrophoenicians, synagogue officials, demoniacs, children, lepers, people with hemmorhages, and others who were not permitted to be touched by anybody. Jesus' heart was open for all, and Jesus' church is to be open for all. We cannot claim that He is our head while we maintain exclusiveness because it is the cultural thing to do. The one who is in us is greater than all the differences and diversities of people in the world.

He Is Greater Than God's Special Strokes for Him

At the beginning of Jesus' ministry, God spoke in a way that others could hear, "This is my beloved Son" (Matthew 3:17). On the mount of Transfiguration God repeated that message so that Peter, James, and John could hear (Mark 9:2-8).

Wouldn't it be easy to get big-headed by hearing God honor you in those special ways? Today, several people love to advertise broadly how God has appeared to them and revealed truth to them. In fact, many fund-raising letters are sent across the nation relating that kind of experience.

Jesus never let any of that go to His head. As a matter of fact, when Peter, James, and John heard what the Heavenly Father said about Jesus, Jesus told them not to tell other people about it. He would not allow the special revelations of God about Him to detour Him from becoming humble as a servant for man.

While on the one hand it is tough to live with a lot of criticisms and lack of understandings, it is also tough to live with a lot of recognition, honor, strokes, and privileges. Some people have a tougher time handling the spotlight than handling rejection. Jesus was greater than the spotlights that were turned on Him—even when the spotlight had been flipped on by God himself. The one who is in us is greater than all of the special awards and honors there may be out there in the world, ready to be dumped upon us. Success can make us ineffective as servants. It is not the success that does it, but our attitudes about that success.

He Is Greater Than the Betrayal of Close Friends

It is one thing to be betrayed by those that do not like you. It is something else to be betrayed by those with whom you have been transparent, with whom you have shared those intimate close moments, and with whom you have invested your life.

Jesus' closest friends walked out on Him when the going got tough (Mark 14:10, 27, 50, 66). But Jesus did not carry a grudge. He understood some of what was going on inside of them. He understood their fears. He understood their misunderstandings.

So at the appropriate time, Jesus encountered His disciples again. And He encountered them as friends. He forgave them. He restored their dignity. He cleansed them from guilt. He fellowshiped with them. And He used them. He was willing to walk toward those who walked away from Him. He was willing to pick up those who had dropped Him. And that one who lives in us is greater than the disappointment of our friends in the world.

He Is Greater Than Popularity

Perhaps few things in Jesus' life show His greatness better than His reaction toward popularity. People were amazed at His teaching (Mark 1:23). So what did Jesus do? He immediately did one of those dirty jobs—He healed a leper (Mark 1:23-26). He did not allow their amazement to go to His head. Later we read that all were amazed at Jesus (Mark 1:27). Instead of bathing in that, He went into a private house and ministered to someone with fever (Mark 1:29-31). People began to bring all the sick to Him, because He was becoming quite popular (Mark 1:32). But the next morning, He went out by himself to pray (Mark 1:35). When His apostles came to Him and said, "Everyone is looking for You" (Mark 1:37), Jesus said, "Let us go somewhere else" (Mark 1:38). Jesus was not shy. He went somewhere else because He was not called by God to just take in the popularity, but to preach in as many places as He could.

There was a time when Jesus could not enter publicly into a city (Mark 1:45). When He came into a private home, the crowds flocked so that there was no room in that home (Mark 2:1, 2). But Jesus continued to minister to people's needs amid that popularity (Mark 2:2-13). At times, the crowds were so great that Jesus couldn't eat (Mark 6:31). He was known by the king (Mark 6:14). Wonderful descriptions were given about Him (Mark 6:14, 15; 8:27, 28). On one occasion, when He saw a great crowd beginning to gather, He hurried up a miracle before the crowd could get there—the opposite of what many popular miracle workers would want to do today (Mark 9:25, 26).

One one occasion, He had the whole city in the palm of His hand as they were crying, "Hosanna! Blessed is He who comes in the name of the Lord" (Mark 11:9). He could have taken the city as the new king on that occasion. But had He done so, He would have bypassed the cross. He did not plan those grandstanding events. Many times when He healed someone, He would tell those people not to tell others about it. Jesus didn't do things for standing ovations.

Nor did He get so popular He would go only where there was a guaranteed crowd. It has become so popular today for religious people not to accept engagements unless there is a guaranteed large crowd (with a lot of income). But Jesus was comfortable on a one-to-one basis, in the private homes, and in small gatherings as well as with the multitudes. He was a man for all sizes, as well as for all peoples.

Some of the greatness of Jesus is seen by the fact that He is much bigger than the popularity around Him. And the one who lives in us is greater than all the popularity there is in the world. He expects us to handle that popularity in a way that we don't cave into it—that we don't live for it—that we don't necessarily expect it—that we don't refuse services because the demonstration of popularity is not arranged by our agent or individual planning.

He Is Greater Than Death

He healed the dead, although laughed at (Mark 5:35-43). And He went to the cross because He knew that we were all dying in our sins. On the cross, He became greater than our individual deaths, for He took those deaths into himself. And through the cross, He became greater than His own death, for He arose from the grave after a devastating execution.

The one who is in us is greater than the death that is in the world. That's why Paul wrote to those Christians in Rome (many of whom were facing death) these words, "For I am convinced that neither death, nor life, nor angels, nor principalities, nor things present, nor things to come, nor powers, nor height, nor depth, nor any other created thing, shall be able to separate us from the love of God, which is in Christ Jesus our Lord" (Romans 8:38, 39).

In Christ, a person passes from death to life. In Christ, physical death is not just an exodus from this life, it is also an arrival to be with the Lord. In Christ, there is no condemnation. For the Christian, physical death is a transition—never a termination.

The Christians at Rome who were facing violent death needed to hear that. And so do we!

He Is Greater Than Resurrection

How can Jesus be greater than resurrection? That is because Jesus is not great because of the resurrection, but the resurrection is great because of Jesus. Other people have had resurrections, but they have died again. Jesus' resurrection is great because He is eternal. He will never die again.

After He arose, the angel's message to the disciples was this: "He is going before you into Galilee" (Mark 16:7). That message is still ours today. Jesus has gone before us—not into Galilee, but into Heaven to prepare a place for us. He arose to live forever.

The angel's message also said, "You will see Him." And that message is still for us. John wrote, "Beloved, now we are children of God, and it has not appeared as yet what we shall be. We know that, when He appears, we shall be like Him, because we shall see Him just as He is" (1 John 3:2).

After Jesus arose and appeared before His disciples, He reclined at the table with them. And He will recline at a table with us. It is going to be a wedding banquet. At that time there will be celebration.

> And I heard, as it were, the voice of a great multitude and as the sound of many waters and as the sound of mighty peals of thunder, saying,
> "Hallelujah! For the Lord our God, the Almighty, reigns. Let us rejoice and be glad and give the glory to Him, for the marriage of the Lamb has come and His bride has made herself ready." And it was given to her to clothe herself in fine linen, bright and clean; for the fine linen is the righteous acts of the saints. And he said to me, "Write, 'Blessed are those who are invited to the marriage supper of the Lamb.'" And he said to me, "These are true words of God" (Revelation 19:6-9).

After Jesus' resurrection, He commissioned His disciples to go into all the world and preach the gospel to every person. And that commission is still His marching orders for us today.

In addition to those marching orders is the promise of His presence and His power. Some people use the promises of Jesus to those apostles in Mark 16:18 as an excuse to throw up tests to Jesus. They purposely pick up deadly snakes and drink poison in an exhibitionist kind of way to prove they are disciples of Jesus. But that is not the context of Jesus' promise. He promises extraordinary provisions while His people are in the activities of evangelizing the nations. The nations involved enemy, alien, contradictory, and oppositional people and territories. Who wants to do that unless the presence of the risen Lord is promised? While we normally like to keep those promises of Jesus trapped in the first century, many missionaries have experienced that extraordinary presence of the Lord during those tough times. Many missionaries can testify that they lived through experiences that should normally have killed them. Jesus never promised that He would so protect His people that they would never be hurt, harmed, or killed physically. Everyone of those apostles died. All of them but one died at the hands of their enemies.

What Jesus was really promising was that when His disciples are making His mission a priority, then they will not do it alone, "Lo, I am with you always, even to the end of the age" (Matthew 28:20). To assume that this means everything will always be peaches and cream is to forget that Jesus himself went to the cross.

The real power of Jesus' resurrection is not to be restricted to the temporary sensational provisions, but includes having the inner presence of Jesus and thus the presence of His power inside of us to face life, sufferings, and death the way He did. It is to have the presence of His character making a difference in the way we live.

That is what Paul meant when he said that he wanted to be found in Christ having "the righteousness which comes from God on the basis of faith, that I may know Him, and the power of His resurrection and the fellowship of His sufferings, being conformed to His death; in order that I may attain to the resurrection from the dead" (Philippians 3:9-11). Paul elsewhere made it clear that to experience Christ's resurrection is to experience a newness in the quality of the way we live here and now—freed from slavery to sin and liberated to become not just sons, but also slaves of God himself (Romans 6:5-14).

We have already tasted a resurrection if we are in Christ. The first resurrection happened when we arose with Christ to walk in a newness of life (Romans 6:4). That newness of life is possible because God puts within us His Holy Spirit. That Holy Spirit equips us with a standard for Christlike living. We don't reach Christlikeness instantly. It is an ongoing process. And God expects progress in that process. He expects His children to be growing toward maturity.

Sometimes our progress is hindered because we allow the difficult, dark, dismal, and damaging events around us to drain our energy, detour our priorities, and dampen the Holy Spirit within us.

The Christians in Rome, going through devastating times, needed to be reminded that they were to take their eyes off the raunchy stuff happening to them and put their eyes onto the resurrection of Jesus, who is alive and well on planet earth and who empowered them.

They needed look to the future, not just be paralyzed to the present. They needed to reach out toward the goal ahead of them.

Not only must *they* have done it, but *we* must do it also—here and now!

That is possible because Christ is greater than a resurrection that happened two thousand years ago. He is greater because the resurrection happened once and for all then, but Christ continues to exist now. He is alive! He is present! And He dwells within the Christians! And because He is in us, He expects us to press on while events may be trying to press us in. He expects us to lay hold of life. He wants us to reach out. He wants us to reach forward and let go of what has gone on in the past.

That's possible because the power of the resurrection is the power of the risen Christ living in us. That's what Paul meant when he said that there is far more to life than the past and the present. And he was reaching out for it:

> Not that I have already obtained it, or have already become perfect, but I press on in order that I may lay hold of that for which also I was laid hold of by Christ Jesus. Brethren, I do not regard myself as having laid hold of it yet; but one thing I do: forgetting what lies behind and reaching forward to what lies ahead, I press on toward the goal for the prize of the upward call of God in Christ Jesus (Philippians 3:12-14).

So let us declare together, "Throw what you will at us, Life. We admit that we live in a Rome of our day, but nevertheless, we press on toward the prize of the upward call of God in Christ Jesus."